The Islands of Destiny

The Islands of Destiny

W I L L I A M   W A L K E R

Order this book online at www.trafford.com
or email orders@trafford.com

Most Trafford titles are also available at major online book retailers.

Printed in the United States of America.

ISBN: 978-1-4269-6010-9 (sc)
ISBN: 978-1-4269-6011-6 (e)

Library of Congress Control Number: 2011903448

Trafford rev. 03/03/2011

 www.trafford.com

North America & International
toll-free: 1 888 232 4444 (USA & Canada)
phone: 250 383 6864 ♦ fax: 812 355 4082

"Wherefore glory ye the Lord of the fires, even the name of the Lord God of Israel in the isles of the sea.

From the uttermost <u>part</u> of the earth have we heard songs, even glory to the righteous....."

(The Holy Bible – Isaiah 24: 15-16)

CONTENTS

ILLUSTRATIONS

Preface

The purpose I have for writing this book is that a true history may be preserved of 'The Birth of the Anglo-Saxon-Celtic Nations.' Especially the inhabitants of the British Isles and Ireland, and to explain the meaning of the writings of Isaiah in connection with this history.

Every word of God's Book is in its right place. It may sometimes seem to us to be deranged. The Lock may be in one place and the Key may sometimes be hidden away elsewhere in some apparently inadvertent word or sentence. A volume might be written in illustration of this fact, and it would be a profitable Bible or Scripture Study to seek out these 'Keys' which explain the seemingly inexplicable, perplexing statements in certain books of the Bible, and by certain Prophets. Statements which seem to contradict other 'known facts', and which are used by unbelievers to justify their claims that the Scriptures are not inspired.

One such perplexing statement is that which is made by Isaiah in chapter 24 verses 15-16 from which the title of this book was chosen.

Isaiah does not give any indication to whom he is referring to in this statement, and he gives no explanation in the verses that follow. It is a statement which comes completely 'out of the blue.'

Whilst most Scriptural Locks have a Scriptural Key, there are some Locks that are more difficult and require a combination of Keys. Some in Scriptural Books, and others in Secular History; Isaiah 24:15-16 is one such Lock. The Lock is a combination one, and a seemingly difficult one at that! Many students of Isaiah have searched for the 'Master Key' to unlock his statements – leaving us only with opinions – BUT NOW THE MASTER KEY HAS BEEN FOUND – not in Biblical books or Scriptures, but in 'Chronicles of History', which have rested in the Archives of the British Library for many years gathering the dust of time – waiting for their re-discovery. I refer to the 'Chronicles of Eri':- being the 'History of the Gaal Sciot Iber' – or 'The Irish People', translated from the original manuscripts in the 'Phoenician Dialect of the Scythian Language' by Dr. Roger O'Connor in 1822 AD! Also the 'National Triads of Wales', which are, according to Matthew Arnold and Professor Max Muller, 'The Oldest Literature in the Oldest Living Language of Europe'.

This 'Oldest (Celtic) Literature' is the 'Historic Triads of the Island of Britain' of which one hundred and sixty are still in existence. They consist of 'The Poems of Ancient Bards', and convey to us the Religion, Philosophy, and Law of the Early Britons. Like the Ancient Vedas of India, they were handed down by oral tradition, and not until the sixth century AD were they written down by the 'Bards of King Arthur's Court', Taliesin and Llynwarch Hen, when the British King re-organised the 'Old Order' on Christian lines, and drew up his 'Rules of the Round Table' on 'The Druidic Principles of Loyalty and Self Sacrifice to King and Country'. Information regarding the colonization of Britain gathered principally from these Triads, and Druidic remains were collected by the (late) Welsh Scholar and Bard – REV. R W MORGAN.

In this ancient literature concerning the Primitive Migrations of the KYMRY (Welsh), is to be found one of the oldest traditions of the Flood, in the days of NOAH, which I will quote later.

There are many other ancient books of history which provide further keys in our search, however, the quotations and references from these will be used in their connection with the 'Chronicles of Eri' and the 'Triads of Wales'. In particular I mention the 'Old British Chronicles' – these are handed down to us through Latin Translations made by the Christian British Scholars – GILDAS ALBANIUS, of the 5th Century AD, NENNIUS, of the 9th Century AD, and Bishop Geoffrey of Monmouth who lived about 1150 AD. Geoffrey's version was translated from the Latin into English by A. Thompson of Oxford in 1718 AD, and reproduced by J. Giles into Modern English.

Of course the purpose of this book is to draw your attention towards my country Britain and the British Isles, including Ireland, in a completely new way. It is coupled with the aim to arouse interest in a completely new approach to the 'Writings of Isaiah'! I hope I can plant a seed which will flourish and take root in the minds of seekers of the truth.

In the words of Paul:-

> *'I have planted, Apollos watered, but God gave the increase. So then neither is he that planteth anything, neither he that watereth, but God giveth the increase. Now he that planteth and he that watereth are one, and every man shall receive his own reward according to his labour.*
>
> *For we are labourers together with God .... I have laid the foundation, and another buildeth thereon. But let every man take heed how he buildeth thereupon.*
>
> *For other foundation can no man lay than that is laid, which is Jesus Christ.'*

(1 Cor. 3: 6-11)

As such then this study is only a start.

A Personal Experience

My personal belief is that the daily events of one's life are just cogs in the 'Wheel of Destiny', when one is cognisant that God controls our destiny. In 1967 whilst on holiday in Cornwall, I read a booklet which purported to identify Britain and the British people with the so called 'Ten Lost Tribes in Israel' that disappeared in Assyrian captivity. That booklet planted a seed in me that became a quest similar to the search for the 'Holy Grail'. In my quest I was continually reading references to the ancient 'Chronicles of Eri' previously mentioned. Upon making enquiries at the local library in Lowestoft, I was informed that these were rare books, and as such would only be available from the British Library Document Supply Centre, Boston Spa, Weatherby, West Yorkshire, UK, LS23 7BQ. The librarian at Lowestoft requested copies of the two volumes, which duly arrived, and which I have obtained on many occasions since 1970 in order to collate the information presented in 'The Islands of Destiny' (Ref: Re James B HAGGART). I have since discovered that in all probability there are only, no more than, three complete sets of these 'Ancient Chronicles' still in existence in the world. One set I know of is held in a private collection in the USA. Therefore I do hope that my book will re-kindle a renewed interest, and requests for the 'Chronicles' may result in a new edition being printed.

Although I commenced collecting the resource material for this book in 1970, and making extensive research of the 'Chronicles', it seems as though the time was not ripe until now for the world to receive the light that they offer.

Trying to launch a new idea, unheard of by most readers, it is difficult to make a choice from the vast storehouses of wisdom existing in the British

Libraries about the Anglo-Saxon-Celtic peoples - being descended from the 'Ancient <u>House</u> of Israel' (Ten Tribes), as distinguished from the Jews (remnants of the '<u>House</u> of Judah'), and the '<u>KINGDOM</u> OF ISRAEL' (ALL TWELVE TRIBES)(not to be identified with the modern Jewish 'STATE OF ISRAEL') – that I must endorse my appreciation for the wonderful British Library organization and the assistance I have been given in locating all the books I required. No effort was spared by my local library to help in every way possible. In what follows I have only scratched the surface of this enormous amount of material.

Before '<u>THE LIGHT</u>' returns to the earth, we have to know ourselves and our identities, not only as individuals, but also as a people.

Readers must keep in mind that the subject matter of this book was originally prepared as five separate, two hour lectures, which includes a slide presentation. These five lectures were part of eighty (80), two hour lectures and therefore form only a link in the chain, as all the lectures, although composed of diverse subjects, have a common objective – to bring to light the true identity of the British (Anglo-Saxon-Celtic peoples of the Earth) with the 'House of Israel', and the reason for the restoration of the Gospel in 1820 AD, and the fulfilment of prophecy, especially 'Prophetical Time Measures'.

These lectures were <u>collated</u> and prepared by the author mostly from <u>new</u> material which throw a new and profound light upon Biblical History and Prophecy. They are the result of over twenty two years work, the author being a member of the (Mormon) 'Church of Jesus Christ of Latter-Day Saints' for more than thirty years. However, I hope that this will not prejudice those who are members of other faiths. This work is intended to have no bias – only from the standpoint of those who desire to know the truth and seek further light and knowledge, especially into the writings of Isaiah.

The reader must also try to overlook the rhetoric, as the lectures were prepared for <u>listeners</u> in which the author can also project his personality and demeanour. This will present no problem when the reader knows that the author was a self-employed Salesman and a Sales Executive for most of his professional life, and for many of those years was involved as a Consultant

Training Officer, teaching new Salesmen in Sales and Closing Techniques, therefore the rhetoric became an essential part of the author's personality.

As I have stated earlier – **'I believe the daily events of one's life are just cogs in the Wheel of Destiny'.** I am not suggesting we are pre-ordained to do something or accept a situation that happens to us whether we like it or not, because we all have a free agency to either accept or reject a given course. In this respect I am speaking of fore-ordination, where an opportunity is presented to us – being the way that God wants us to follow – called to His service, but given a choice to either accept or reject that opportunity. In this respect we should not be praying for blessings, but opportunities!

I was born the 23rd November 1922 in Castleford, Yorkshire. That event began the wheel of my destiny. Certain cogs (daily events or decisions) in that wheel changed the course of my life. Some events happened to me which were not of my making, but had a profound influence on my later decisions. The readers will appreciate this remark when I inform them that I joined the 'Royal Navy' as a volunteer in February 1939. I was just sixteen years of age, approaching my seventeenth year. I entered the service as a boy seaman. The Second World War commenced in the September of that year. I completed my Boy Seaman's Training and entered the 'Fleet Service' in 1940. My first experience of the war was joining the Battle Cruiser 'H.M.S London', which was then part of the 'North Atlantic Battle Cruiser Squadron' based at Reykjavik, Iceland.

Sometime later I was transferred to Submarine Service in the Mediterranean area, and at the end of the War was serving in Minesweeping Operations in the Adriatic Sea and off Northern Ireland, based at Londonderry. I completed my active service in February 1948 and then continued to serve in the 'Royal Fleet Reserve' for a further five years.

Why am I telling you this? To show you that all of these events were further cogs in the 'Wheel of my Destiny'. I have written a Journal of my experiences of my early childhood days, and those in the 'Royal Navy' during World War II. I can now look back at those days and see the reason why, on more than one occasion, God has intervened to preserve my life.

In October of 1947 I was stationed in Lowestoft, England, serving on a Fleet Minesweeper 'H.M.S. MARMION'. It was here that I met my sweet wife Freda. We fell in love and were married in Lowestoft on February 21st 1948 (a period of four months). We decided to settle in Leeds, Yorkshire, where there were opportunities for work. However, Freda became homesick for Lowestoft, and I was not too happy in Leeds either, but we had no spare savings for our train fare back. What a dilemma! One Tuesday evening we decided to go out to a hotel to talk things over. The lounge area was practically empty, and we found a quiet spot in the corner. However, it was not long before we were joined at our table by an elderly Jewish gentleman. He asked permission to sit with us. I consented, but I thought to myself – there are all these empty tables and seats and he has to sit here! He visited us for about half an hour, and I must admit I did enjoy his conversation, as I think he did ours. As he left he shook my hand and placed within my palm a small round object – it seemed like a button to me – as it was too small for a coin of the day. He looked me in the eyes, his handshake was warm, his voice full of compassion and he said **"Do not open your hand until I have gone, what I have placed there you have great use for!"** I did as he had said, he departed as quietly as he came. When I opened my hand, there I beheld a gold sovereign! Even in those days they were rare coins, and of great value. I looked at it in amazement. My wife and I were stunned with joy. Here was the answer to our problem, we could now afford the train tickets back to Lowestoft. You will not be surprised to know that when we valued the sovereign at a local jewellers, the value was exactly the price of our train fare! God certainly works in mysterious ways!

We did not become members of the 'Mormon Church' until January 1957. Looking back to the gold sovereign incident I knew, as also did my wife, that it was just another cog in the 'Wheel of Destiny'.

Once again I realised that a – Loving All Wise Creator – had been guiding my life. Of course I could have rejected the opportunity. I could have used the value of the sovereign for a more selfish, materialistic purpose. We had the choice, God presented us with the means and opportunity, but we had the choice! I do honestly believe that the gift of the Gold Sovereign was an

Act of God. Another cog in the Wheel. I could write of hundreds of such incidents, but I feel that in this story my purpose has been achieved.

This book may be a – 'Cog in your Wheel of Destiny' – may it be an opportunity for you to grasp the path which your 'Loving Father in Heaven' would have you follow. For this book will place in your hand something of far greater value than gold.

CHAPTER ONE

The Ancient Chronicles of Eri – An Exposition

What are these Chronicles?

What history do they contain?

The title page to each of these Volumes inform us that the Chronicles contain the History of the GAAL (GAEL) SCIOT IBER.

<u>GAAL</u> or <u>GAEL</u> meaning people or 'Tribe' from which is derived the word 'GAELIC'. The word in Ireland and Scotland means 'CLAN'.

The word <u>SCIOT</u> means in Gaelic – 'Archers' or 'Those proficient in the use of the bow and arrow'. The word SCIOT is today pronounced SCOT. The SCOTS have taken their name from the 'GAEL OF SCIOT IBER' meaning CLAN or CLANS OF IBER, who were famous for their marksmanship in the use of the bow and arrow.

The word <u>IBER</u> – (IB-ER) or (AB-ER) is derived from the name of HEBER or EBER from which we receive the word H-EB-REWS (HEBREWS). It is to be remembered that there were no vowels in the ancient Hebrew Language as opposed to modern Aramaic Hebrew. The vowel sound being applied in the pronunciation of the word. The word 'AB' in Hebrew means 'Father'. Therefore the word AB-ER-EW simply means the Father of the sons, or family of ER, or ERI people.

HEBER was a descendant of SHEM, son of NOAH and was the fourth in this succession of Patriarchs. AB-RAM or AB-RA-HAM being the tenth in this succession of Patriarchs – as given in GENESIS 11: 10-27.

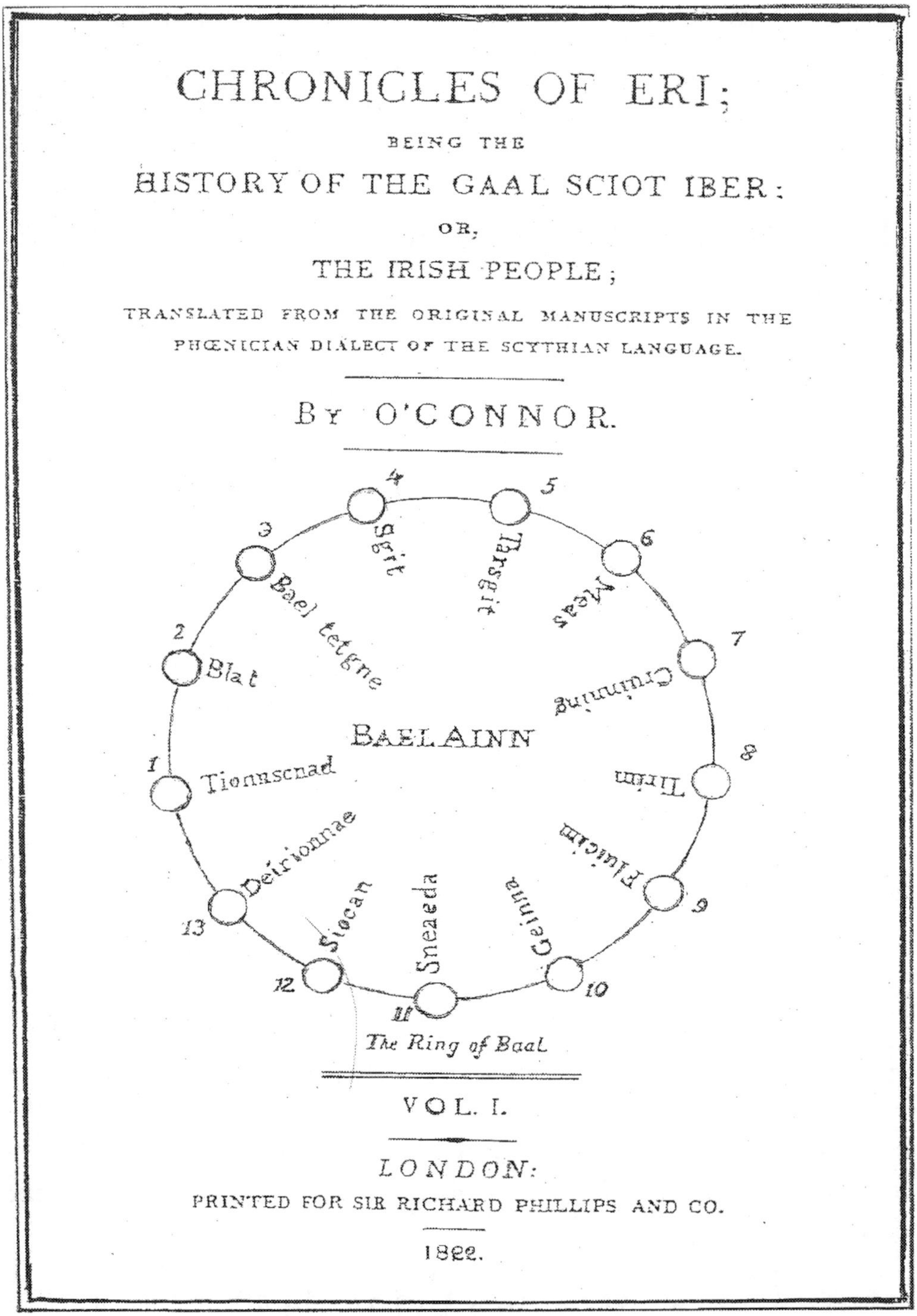

Fig. 1: Chronicles of Eri – Vol. 1

CHRONICLES OF ERI;

BEING THE

HISTORY OF THE GAAL SCIOT IBER:

OR,

THE IRISH PEOPLE;

TRANSLATED FROM THE ORIGINAL MANUSCRIPTS IN THE
PHŒNICIAN DIALECT OF THE SCYTHIAN LANGUAGE.

BY O'CONNOR.

VOL. II.

LONDON:

PRINTED FOR SIR RICHARD PHILLIPS AND CO.

1822.

Fig. 2: Chronicles of Eri – Vol 2

1. SHEM (born before the Flood)

2. ARPHAXAD

3. SELAH

4. EBER (HEBER) (AB-ERI)

5. PELEG

6. REU

7. SERUG

8. NAHOR

9. TERAH

10. AB-RA-HAM (ABRAM)

We are informed in GENESIS 14: 13

> *'And there came one that had escaped and told Abram the Hebrew .....!'*

All the descendants of IB-ER, EB-ER, HEBER became known as HEBREWS or AB-ERI people. All the sons of Abraham, Isaac and Jacob are therefore HEBREWS, **but not Jews**, who descended from the man JUDAH – (JEW-DAH), even so not all of <u>his</u> descendants are called JEWS. JUDAH, the man, had five sons – ER, ONAN, SHELAH, ZARAH, PHAREZ – only a remnant of the line of PHAREZ (who returned from Babylonian captivity were called 'JEWS' (2 KINGS 16: 6).

O'Connor informs us that the Chronicles were translated from the original manuscripts written in the 'PHOENICIAN DIALECT OF THE SCYTHIAN LANGUAGE'. <u>They date from the year of the Flood in the days of NOAH 2400 BC</u>. Therefore the period of the History contained in them is contemporaneous with Biblical History. However, the History contained in the Chronicles <u>concludes in 7 BC</u>.

The Ring of BAAL

The frontispiece of Volume One of 'The Chronicles of Eri' displays 'THE RING OF BAAL'. The name 'Baal' denoting the Sun. The 'Ring' being the ancient 'Scythian – Phoenician Calendar'. In the 'Chronicles', 'Years' are denoted by 'Rings'. It seems as though this 'Ancient Calendar' was divided into Thirteen Periods. O'Connor does not explain this Calendar or how it operated. The reader must not confuse the word 'BAAL' in the 'Chronicles' with that in the Bible where 'BAAL' was a heathen God.

I will include a few verses of the 'Writings of EOLUS' taken from Chapter One of 'The Chronicles', that these may explain the fact.

The Writings of Eolus – Chapter One, Page Four

'How glorious to gain immortality, by having infused a portion of his spirit into the children of man, to abide on the earth forever.

My Son, - Pursue not phantoms of imagination, study thyself – call to mind continually the materials of which thou art composed – if much of them is prone to the sluggishness of earth, the instability of water, the inconsistency of nimble air, remember the fire of thy spirit hath power to control and direct, if thou wilt keep it pure.

Oh! That man should suffer his passions to subdue his reason, the fire of his spirit smothered, all but extinguished, - are earth, air, and water, more powerful than fire? – is matter more potent than spirit?

Why delighteth man to do what he condemneth in another? – Why doth he unto his fellow, what he would not that his fellow should do unto him?

The heart of man is proud – he coveteth power and pre-eminence; he will gain them by deeds of evil, without reflection; he listeneth to the voice of the seducer, the false flattering tongue that betrayeth – unruled passions hurry him on – folly taketh dominion of such an one; reason hath departed from him, his spirit was weak.

My Son, - Let all thy actions be such, that when thy bulk shall be inanimate, thy spirit shall live forever in the hearts of men.

My Son, - Hear the tale of times of old; hear of our race the renowned of earth. What time our Fathers marked not, is as the cloud that hath passed away, no note taken – no memorial preserved.'

The Writings of Eolus – Chapter One, Page Five

'Let us speak of times measured by BAAL in his circuit, as he moveth in his course to animate his children.

How glorious is BAAL, how good, how provident; doth he not produce the fruits that sustain the life of man? – doth he not feed, and warm every living being?

Doth he not give light by day, and impart a portion of his splendour to his dwelling place to illuminate the night, and mark the seasons?

How terrible is BAAL in his anger, when he sendeth forth his messengers in fire, air, and water, and maketh the earth to tremble. All elements are his servants.

<u>Hear of times marked – I have the rings of our fathers; they have noted the rings of their times: I will mark the rings of my days. Thou wilt mark those of thy days – so shall signs and seasons be perpetual.</u>

Attend now, my Son, - Our great fathers dwelt on the left side of the sun's rising, beyond the sources of the great waters. Of days marked whilst BAAL performed one thousand and eleven circuits in his course.

Then did they spread themselves from the flood of Sgeind even to the banks of Teth-gris.

And when one thousand three hundred and four rings were completed, then did our fathers of these days pass to this side of Teth-gris, and moving towards the sun's going, reach to the Affriedg-eis, and they became lords of all the lands on this side.'

The Chronicles

THERE ARE TWO VOLUMES WRITTEN IN THREE PARTS:-

A summary of each part is given by O'Connor in Volume One under 'CONTENTS'.

Following the outline of the 'CONTENTS' in Volume One, O'Connor then provides his readers with what is called a 'Demonstration'; many pages, explaining Historical background, Chronology, Geography, Etymologies, Dates, Facts, Charts, etc., some of which I will include with various Chapters in this book.

The First Volume is headed 'THE WRITINGS OF EOLUS'.

The Second Volume is headed 'THE CHRONICLES OF ERI'.

THE WRITINGS OF EOLUS:- Volume One contains the account of his forefathers from the time of the Flood, 2400 BC, to his own day, 1368 BC. This History is taken from legends and other sources acquired by EOLUS; even so they must be a credible History due to his great integrity and wisdom.

No-one who reads the Chronicles can fail to be impressed by the sincerity of EOLUS.

THE CHRONICLES OF GAEL-AG: Commence with Chapter Six of Volume One

This history records the affairs of the GAAL-SCIOT-IBER in GAEL-AG (GALACIA) in Spain. These are TRUE FACTS being commenced by EOLUS in 1368 BC. And from the time of his death in 1335 BC the history being faithfully recorded by the 'ARD-OLAM' (High Priests) unto 1007 BC in which year the GAAL-SCIOT-IBER migrated from GAEL-AG in Spain to Ireland. <u>This concludes Volume One.</u>

<u>THE CHRONICLES OF ERI: Commence with Volume Two:- are also the TRUE FACTS</u>

Being a continued record of the History of the GAAL-SCIOT-IBER in ERI (Ireland) 1007 BC to 7 BC. After their arrival in Ireland the Sciot of Iber changed their name to GAAL OF ERI, calling their new home ERI. The reason for this change of identity will be explained in Chapter Nine of this book.

Therefore the 'story' contained in the Chronicles cover the History of the GAAL-SCIOT of IBER in three different geographical locations.

<u>PART 1: 2500 BC app. to 1490 BC:-</u>   Deals with the early History of the family of NOAH in ARMENIA and MESOPOTAMIA, Western Asia.

<u>PART 2: 1490 BC to 1007 BC:-</u> Deals with the History of the GAAL-SCIOT-IBER in GAEL-AG of SPAIN.

<u>PART 3: 1007 BC to 7 BC:-</u>   Records the History of the GAAL-SCIOT-IBER under the new name of GAAL-SCIOT-ERI in IRELAND, calling their new name ERI.

Therefore the Chronicles of ERI cover the <u>History of ONE BRANCH OF THE SCYTHIAN HEBREW TRIBES – namely – the EARLY SETTLERS OF IRELAND AND THE BRITISH ISLES</u>, and to trace, not only them, but any Tribes in any way connected with them.

The 'Demonstration Notes' in themselves are a monumental work to O'Connor's knowledge and intelligence. I hope, therefore, that this book will do him proud, due to the great respect I have come to have for him.

READERS PLEASE NOTE

<u>The first Four Chapters and Part One of Chapter Five of this book deal with the Ancient Scythian Civilization, and other migrating colonies of Hebrews to Spain and the British Islands from the year 1800 BC to 1000 BC.</u> This information will prepare you for a better understanding of the History contained in the Chronicles which mainly commence in the days of EOLUS, 1368 BC in Spain.

PLEASE NOTE:-

The main 'Story' of the Chronicles commence with Chapter Five – Part Two of this book.

Dr. Roger O'Connor (Part One)

In my opinion to know the book, especially one of such magnitude as the 'Chronicles of Eri', and as such, creating a diversity of opinions, I think, therefore, it is best that we get to know a little about the author.

As with all great men, O'Connor has his critics. As with all new truth, some accept it immediately, some reject it, claiming it to be a forgery or 'fruits of the imagination'.

Jesus Christ himself had his critics, he was accused of teaching false doctrines – working miracles by the power of Baalzebub. He was rejected and crucified by his own kin.

Joseph Smith the 'Mormon Prophet' also has been accused of practically every wicked offence. He and his family and followers were persecuted, and are still persecuted and misunderstood, especially being accused of being non-Christian.

The Book of Mormon also having its critics. Those who claim it to be a forgery, and yet others who bear witness that it is the work and revelation of God.

As you will see O'Connor was no exception, neither were the Chronicles.

Firstly then, let us see what O'Connor looked like. Fortunately a print of a photograph was placed in the first page of Volume One of the Chronicles – which is reproduced here!

PORTRAIT OF DR. ROGER O'CONNOR 1820 A.D.

Dͬ Roger O'Connor

1820

Fig. 3: Portrait of Dr Roger O'Connor 1820 A.D

Dr. Roger O'Connor (Part Two)

<u>Firstly</u>:- I enclose a copy of a letter written by O'Connor to his trusted friend Sir Francis Burdett of FORMARK (BARONET) M.P (undated), but must have been penned by O'Connor sometime in 1820 AD

<u>Secondly</u>:- I will enclose a copy of O'Connor's Preface to Volume One of the Chronicles.

<u>Thirdly</u>:- O'Connor's Biography as given in the Dictionary of National Biography Volume Fifteen – page 852/3.

<u>Finally</u>:- A remark made in a letter sent to me in reply to an enquiry from the Assistant Librarian, Manuscripts Department, Trinity College Library, Dublin.

<u>Sir Francis Burdett</u> – of Formark, Baronet

My Friend,

When in accordance with my desire that you should have the evidence of your own senses, wherefrom to form your own judgement of the length, depth, and complexion of the last conspiracy against my life and honour, by agents of an oligarchy, whose every act is working a mighty revolution in all the countries subject, and subjected to their fell dominion, you came to Ireland; at which time you consulted me as to the best account of my ill-fated country; I requested of you to content yourself for the present with reading the book that lay open before you, the dimensions thereof wide as the land, whereon you would see marks of the iron-hand of despotism; the time of pressure to be calculated from the woeful havoc it had made; and I promised that it would, as soon as could be, present you with a true and faithful history of my country, from the earliest times, which would clearly explain those causes that had produced the effects you sympathetically deplored.

I now come, late as to time, but, as you know, quickly, when the manifold afflictions and consequent ill-health under which I laboured, are taken into account, <u>to fulfil the promise I then made; not to lay at your feet, but to place in your hands, the most ancient Chronicles of the people</u> whose descendants you saw, and whose melancholy condition brought many a tear from your manly pitying eye.

<u>In selecting you as executor of this legacy which I bequeath to those that now be, and to those who are yet to come, for an everlasting possession,</u> it is necessary that I tell posterity the reason that hath actuated me to commit to you this trust, which is not to be found in the exemplary manner in which you have carried yourself in all the relations of private life; nor because of your acquirements in the walks of literature; nor in the many proofs I have had of your friendship through a series of nearly thirty years; nor yet for the extension of your full and fostering hand towards my children, whom you have made partakers of a portion of your wealth, since persecution, in varied shapes, and the success of diabolical machinations of a perfidious traitor, taking advantage of the situation in which I had been placed by that persecution, had deprived their father of the means.

Had it not been for you, my gallant boy, into whose hands you gave his first sword, with instructions how to use the destroying weapon in support of the rights of man, against tyranny and oppression, tempering justice with mercy; into whose ear you poured lessons of wisdom, precepts of humanity; - had it not been for you, the career of glory, wherein his actions have shed additional lustre even on our names, had been cut short, and he had been deprived of his fair proportion of the renown of these brave warriors who have established the <u>independence of the republic of Columbia,</u> all of whom *are loud in his praise. Even these powerful causes united, would not be of sufficient weight to induce me to constitute you the trustee of such a charge; these things appertain to private life, and I feel pride in proclaiming to the world my thanks therefore.*

These reasons and many more to combine to cause me to admire you, to have an affection for you, and to retain a friendship for you of a nature which few but faithful Irishmen can feel; which when sincere, nothing can destroy, though a tremendous blast may shake; its position regained, when founded on a rock, as my friendship is for you.

My motive is, that having had opportunities, <u>for seven and twenty years</u>, of knowing you to the core, having studied you, having watched you with an eye of circumspection and of a true friend, who would have found fault if he saw cause, I cannot call to my recollection one act in your relation with the public that I do not approve, I cannot think on any one occasion, that you have betrayed the trust reposed in you by them; whilst your never-failing <u>advocacy</u> and vindication of the Irish people, has endeared you to all our hearts.

At sometimes you have said, that it was most discouraging to attempt to improve the condition of the state; you have compared the inutility of your continued efforts to the constant drawing up of empty buckets from a well; pardon me, Sir, be assured the buckets you have drawn up, have not been empty;- nay, they have been brim-full, and the people are refreshing themselves with the contents. Tis true, your eloquence and the proclamation of your just principles, have made no impression on the self-nominated and predetermined assembly of St. Stephens, amongst whom the rule is, that what they call private honour, should supersede public duty; but not so with the people; the sentiments you have uttered within the walls of that house, have been disseminated far and wide, and produced enquiries tending to the most beneficial results for your country, to promote the true <u>interests</u> of which, your labours have been unceasing.

Your name is identified with the history of your times;- a majestic column is erecting to perpetuate the memory of Burdett of Formark.

May long time pass before it is completed; and when completed, it will be of the most chaste and simple order, all its members in perfect correspondence, the characters in the universal language of nature, speaking to all the nations of the earth.

Behold the reward of a grateful people, to the incorruptible Patriot, the just Steward, the true faithful Representative, the eloquent Orator, the intrepid Assertor of the liberties of mankind, the MAN who dared to be honest in the worst of times, and who scorned to court that popular applause, which it was his chiefest ambition to deserve!

I am, Sir,

With sincere respect for your many virtues,

Your faithful friend,

O'CONNOR

Sir Francis Burdett of Formark (Baronet) M.P eventually had O'Connor's translation of the Chronicles published in 1822 – obviously he was a true and loyal friend!

<u>Preface</u>

<u>This is the fourth effort</u> which I have made, to present to the world a faithful history of my country.

Whilst I was immured in a prison in Dublin, during parts of the years 1798 and 1799, charged by the oligarchy of England with the foul crime of treason, <u>because I would not disgrace my name by the acceptance of an earldom and a pension</u>, to be paid by the people whom I was courted to desert, and because I resisted their every art to induce me to become a traitor to my beloved Eri, I employed my time in writing a history of that ill-fated land, <u>which I had brought down to a very late period</u>, when an armed force of Buckinghamshire militia men entered my prison, and all the result of my labours, <u>with such ancient manuscripts as I had then by me, were outrageously taken away, and have never since been recovered</u>.

Having been removed from Dublin in March 1799, and taken off to Fort George in Scotland, in the very teeth of the provisions of the Habeas Corpus Act, because I would not become a party to a compromise, whereby I should have destroyed my own fame, and justified the multitudinous acts of tyranny exercised towards me; <u>in that military fortress I was occupied, when health permitted, in again writing the history of my native land, which I had brought down to the last moment that I remained in that part of Scotland, where I was detained until the commencement of 1801, and from whence I was brought away a prisoner</u>.

A part of my family and myself reached **Forres**, the first night after our departure, and the ladies having left their muffs in the room of the Inn in which we sat, they found on the succeeding morning that the messenger had ripped the linings, under the suspicion, no doubt, of communications from my fellow prisoners to their friends, whom I had left behind, being there secreted, in ignorance that I had given an assurance to Governor Stewart, that neither I, nor any of my family, would be the bearers of any papers from them.

This occurrence, added to the circumstances of my manuscripts having been accidentally left behind at Meldrum, for which I had to send back a few miles, made my family apprehensive that if the messenger should lay his hands upon them, my captivity would be prolonged; and having passed a day of festivity at Aberdeen, with the officers and wives of a regiment of native Scots, who had been quartered at Fort George, during a part of the time of my abode there, and from whom my family and myself had experienced something more warm than mere attention; the scene brought back to our recollection days of former times, and the partner of my secret thoughts being entitled to command *any sacrifice that she would ask, having requested of me to suffer her to commit my writings to the flames, I could not do otherwise than yield; thus perished the fruits of my labour in Fort George.*

Having regained my liberty shortly after my arrival in London, so far as going abroad, I did not resume my favourite object during my abode in England, which was *till 1803, when I returned to my own country, and having availed myself of the earliest opportunity of reclaiming from the bowels of the earth the most Ancient Manuscripts of the History of Eri, I recommenced my pursuit upon a more enlarged scale, and had completed the work down to the memorable era of 1315, since Christ,* (**when the five Kings of Eri**, *laying aside their jealousies, invited Edward Bruce, a prince of their own race, to accept of the sovereignty of the land), when it, and almost all my most valuable effects, to a great amount, perished in the flames which consumed all but the bare walls of the castle of Dangan, in the year 1809.*

Were I a fatalist, assuredly I would have thought that it had been decreed, that an authentic history of Inisfail, the Isle of Destiny, was never to see the light. Having, for some time afterwards, been kept fully occupied by agents of the oligarchy of England, in defending my property and life;- liberty we wild Irish have none to lose, *I, for a while, abandoned my project, and until the arrival of Sir Francis Burdett in Ireland in 1817,* meant to defer its execution; when I promised to present to him, at as early a day as possible, an history of Ireland on the truth of which he could rely; which promise I now fulfil. *This history is a literal translation into the English tongue, (from the Phoenician dialect of the Scythian language), of the*

Ancient Manuscripts which have, fortunately for the world, been preserved through so many ages, chances and vicissitudes.

Should any captious person be inclined to entertain suspicion of the antiquity of these manuscripts, I beg leave to observe, that I do not presume to affirm that the very skins, whether of sheep or of goats, are of a date so old as the events recorded; *but this I will assert, that they must be faithful transcripts from the most ancient records; it not being within the range of possibility, either from their style, language, or contents, that they could have been forged.*

So fully sensible was a man of Ireland, who far surpassed all his contemporaries, and in truth, most men, I allude to **Henry Flood,** *that if encouragement were given to bring to light and investigate Ancient Records of Ireland, still existing, they would be the means of diffusing great knowledge of the Antique World; and which, with the Memorials of the East that even still remain, would illuminate all the intermediate spaces of the earth; so convinced was he, I say, of this fact, by means of the deep researches which his penetrating mind had made, that he bequeathed the whole of his large possessions for the purpose of instituting professorships in the University of Dublin, for the perpetuation of the Irish Language, and the purchase of Manuscripts therein.* In this magnificent design, his views were unfortunately frustrated by the contemptible policy of the incubus that hath long over-lain unhappy Eri; for, a claimant was set up to the estates of the philosophic donor, to whom they were accordingly **decreed!** *Had his bequest been suffered to take effect, there is no doubt but that very many Manuscripts, of Great Antiquity and value, which now are mouldering in a neglected state, would have been brought forth.*

It is not possible, nor would it be proper if it were, to anticipate exceptions which peradventure, may be taken to the 'Chronicles of Eri'. If such, however, should be made, and of value sufficient, the objectors may rely upon it, that satisfactory answers shall be given to all doubts and suspicions, which hitherto have invariably been found to be proportionate with the ignorance which at this moment pervades the people of England, with regard to the History, Ancient and Modern, of this celebrated land,- once the Seat of Learning, and Equal and Just Laws, now of demoralization and injustice.

It remains that I now acquaint the world, that I shall instantly resume my work for the purpose of continuing the History of Eri, *the next volume of which, to* *be brought down to the year of the Christian era, 1169; I hope to complete so as to be ready for publication in the month of March next; and if I live, I will prepare the Chronicles of Ireland to the day of my birth in another volume, and then I will give the History of my Own Times in one other, the Concluding Volume of the whole; which **Five Volumes** will be a complete continued History of this Noble Island, under the names of Eri, to the year **1169**, and of Ireland from that epoch, from the most remote time to the instant on which I shall drop my pen.*

O'CONNOR

Paris, 1821.

According to the concluding remarks O'Connor intended to write Five Volumes:-

Volume One – 'From the Year of the Flood to 1008 BC.'

Volume Two – '1008 BC to 7 BC'

Volume Three – '7 BC to 1169 AD'

Volume Four – '1169 AD to the Day of O'Connor's **Birth** 1762'

Volume Five – 'The Concluding Volume:-

The History of His Own Times From 1762 AD to 1834 AD'.

We only have Volumes One and Two!

O'Connor does not identify where he obtained the 'Original Scythian Manuscript', but reading between the lines it seems to have been found amongst others in the 'Archives of the University of Dublin'. To which a trusted intellectual friend HENRY FLOOD bequeathed the whole of his large possessions for the purpose of instituting professorships and the purchasing of other manuscripts therein. What light would these shed I wonder?

I can only conclude therefore that the 'Original Ancient Manuscripts' on which the 'Chronicles' were written and discovered by O'Connor were lost in the fire at 'Dangan Castle' as O'Connor testifies in the Preface, and that no other such 'Manuscripts' of similar nature have been uncovered in the 'Archives of the Libraries in Dublin', of which O'Connor states that had HENRY FLOOD'S bequest taken effect:-

> 'There is no doubt but that very many Manuscripts, of Great Antiquity and value, which now are mouldering in a neglected state, would have been brought forth.....that they would be the means of diffusing great knowledge of the antique world'.

Therefore, like the 'Book of Mormon', we only have the <u>translation</u> of these 'Ancient Manuscripts of the GAAL SCIOT OF IBER'.

It will be noticed that Roger's portrait is pre-fixed, described as:-

'O'CONNOR CIER-RIGE HEAD OF HIS RACE'!

and

'O'CONNOR CHIEF OF THE PROSTRATED PEOPLE OF THIS NATION'

'SOUMIS PAS – VAINCUS'

These titles of course are self imposed, placed there in my opinion by O'Connor as a gesture of defiance toward the British Authorities, due to his refusal at one time –

> <u>'because I would not disgrace my name by the acceptance of an earldom and a pension, to be paid by the people whom I was courted to desert, and because I resisted their every art to induce me to become a traitor to my beloved Eri'.</u>

This refusal to accept a British Earldom, and betray his people, (as he puts it) – must have incensed the British Authorities, and according to O'Connor was the cause of him being arrested on the trumped up charges of treason, and placed in prison in Dublin during the years 1798-1799, where he employed his time in writing '**an History of Ireland to a very late date** – when an armed force of Buckinghamshire Militiamen entered my prison, and all the results of my labours, WITH SUCH ANCIENT MANUSCRIPTS AS I HAD THEN BY ME, were outrageously taken away, and have never since been recovered'.

From the prison in Dublin O'Connor was transferred to a Military Fortress – Fort George – near Inverness in Scotland ..... where he was detained until 1801 AD. He then informs us that he returned to Ireland in 1803 AD to reclaim – '**from the bowels of the earth** the most Ancient Manuscripts of the History of Eri'.

Upon reading these accounts contained in the Preface, one can understand the reasons for O'Connor's defiant attitude, and even moreso for his self imposed titles to his portrait.

Dictionary of National Biography – Volume XV English Edition

O'CONNOR, ROGER (1762 – 1834), Irish Nationalist, born at Connorville, co. Cork, in 1762, was son of Roger Connor of Connorville by Anne, daughter of Robert Longfield, MP (1688 – 1765), and sister of Richard Longfield, <u>created Viscount Longueville in 1800. The Connor family was descended from a rich London Merchant</u>, and its claims to Ancient Irish descent are very doubtful. Arthur O'Connor (q.v.) was Roger's brother. <u>Roger entered the University of Dublin in 1777, and joined the English Bar in 1784</u>. His early bias was in favour of the old Tory regime; as a young man he entered the Muskerry Yeomanry, and helped to hunt down 'Whiteboys'.

He soon, however, changed his views, <u>and joined the United Irishman</u>. In 1797 a warrant left Dublin Castle for his arrest, at the instance of his own brother Robert. He was imprisoned at Cork, <u>was tried and acquitted</u>. On his liberation in April 1798 he went to London, with the intention, as he says, of 'residing there and avoiding any interference in politics'; <u>but his brother Arthur had just been arrested at Margate, and the Home Office decided on again securing Roger. He was sent</u>

from place to place in the custody of King's messengers, and on 9th June 1798 was finally committed to Newgate in Dublin.

In April 1799, with his fellow-prisoners, T.A. Emmet, Chambers, his brother Arthur, and others, he was removed to Fort George in Scotland. In the same year he managed to publish 'Letters to the People of Great Britain'.

After some years' imprisonment he obtained his release. His affairs had been ruined meanwhile, but he had fortune enough to rent Dangan Castle, Trim, Co. Meath. The house was burnt down shortly after he had effected an insurance on it for £5000. He then eloped with a married lady, and in 1817 was arrested at Trim for having headed a band of his retainers in robbing the Galway coach. The son of O'Connor's agent asserted that this raid was made by O'Connor not for money, but in quest of a packet of love-letters, written by his friend Sir Francis Burdett, and which were likely to be used in evidence against Burdett at the suit of a peer who suspected him of criminal intimacy with his wife. *Sir Francis Burdett hurried to Ireland as a witness on O'Connor's behalf at his trial at Trim, and Roger was acquitted.*

In 1822 O'Connor published 'The Chronicles of Eri', being the 'History of the Gael, Sciot Iber', or 'Irish People': translated from the Original Manuscripts in the Phoenician dialect of the Scythian Language. *The book is mainly, if not entirely, the fruit of O'Connor's imagination.* Roger's portrait is prefixed, described as 'O'Connor Cier-rige, Head of His Race', and 'O'Connor, Chief of the Prostrated People of this Nation'. 'Soumis, Pas Vaincus'. O'Connor is described as a man of fascinating manners and conversation, but Dr. Madden considers that his wits were always more or less disordered. Through life he professed to be a sceptic in religion, and declared that Voltaire was his God. *He died at Kilcrea, Co. Cork, on 27 Jan 1834.*

His will, a strange document, beginning: 'I O'Connor and O'Connor Cier-rige, called by the English, Roger O'Connor, late of Connorville and Dangan Castle' is dated 1 July 1831.

Feargus O'Connor (q.v.), the chartist, was his son.

(O'Connor's 'Letters to the People of Great Britain', etc., Dublin, 1799: Pelham MSS., Brit-Mus; Fitzpatrick's Secret Service under Pitt, 1892; Dublin and London Mag. 1828, p.30; information from Professor Barry, Queen's College, Cork (son of Roger's agent); Madden's United Irishmen; Ireland before the Union).

W.J.F.

Letter to Assistant Librarian – Manuscripts Department – Trinity College, Dublin 23rd August 1988

My letter to:- The Librarian of the Manuscripts Department, Trinity College, Dublin, requesting information about 'The Chronicles' and 'Roger O'Connor's Biography'. Also specifically asking if it was possible for similar 'Ancient Phoenician Manuscripts' to be in existence in the Archives of the Libraries in Dublin. The answer to this question was avoided. The reply to my letter was dated 5th September 1988. It was as follows:-

Trinity College Library, Dublin

William Scott Walker

109 Yarmouth Road

Lowestoft

Suffolk

NR32 4AF   5 September 1988

Dear Mr Walker

Thank you for your letter of 23 August.

<u>In the climate of the early 19th Century it was possible for the 'Chronicles of Eri' to be passed off as 'history'. I would judge that 'forgery', rather than legend, is what it really is!</u>

There are many books available concerning the History of Ireland. There is a series called the Gill History of Ireland and another series called the Helicon History of Ireland and the standard work is the New History of Ireland (but that has not been fully published yet). <u>When you have a good idea of the History of Ireland you can judge how worthwhile it is to tell your faculty about the Legends, and the Forged Legends, of Ireland.</u> Dr. Roger O'Connor's Biography is available in the Dictionary of National Biography.

Le meas

Assistant Librarian

Manuscripts Department

A Strange Parallel (Part Three)

What comparisons can we draw from O'Connor's experiences, and the comments related in the Biography, and other sources?

The comments about to be made do offer 'A STRANGE PARALLEL', and will be appreciated more by those readers who are members of the 'Mormon Church', or by those acquainted with a True History of the Church – Joseph Smith, and the 'Book of Mormon'.

There is a strange parallel between the life, times, and experiences of Roger O'Connor and the 'Chronicles of Eri', and Joseph Smith and the 'Book of Mormon', which cannot be coincidence. If something happens once, it can be said it is an accident. If twice, a coincidence, but if it happens three times or more, then it is a fact.

It Seems Strange That:-

1. The 'Ancient Manuscripts of the Chronicles of Eri' should come into the possession of Dr. O'Connor in the years 1798/9 – just a few years before Joseph Smith received his first vision relating to the 'Book of Mormon'. And at the commencement of the Lunar Millenium 1820 AD.

2. That O'Connor had to hide the 'Original Manuscripts' of the 'Chronicles' **'in the bowels of the earth'** to prevent them falling into the wrong hands. In a similar way in which the 'Gold Plates' containing the record of the 'Ancient Civilisation of the Americas' were hidden, about 400 AD by

Moroni – Son of Mormon. And how on other occasions Joseph Smith had to hide the 'Plates' and 'Manuscript' from those who opposed his work.

3. That O'Connor made four attempts to translate the 'Chronicles' – in a similar way that Joseph Smith had to wait four years to obtain the 'Plates of Mormon', before his work could commence.

4. That O'Connor did not complete his work until 1822 AD. Just about two years before the coming forth of the 'Book of Mormon'.

5. It took O'Connor twenty four years, all told, to complete the work of translating the 'Chronicles' – (commencing in 1798 AD and completing in 1822 AD), his Manuscripts being destroyed or lost four times in various ways. At least twice being destroyed by British Militia, and at one time, being burned by O'Connor to prevent them falling into the wrong hands. Eventually he passed from this life on the 27th January 1834 AD.

   In a similar way Joseph Smith took twenty four years to complete his work and mission – commencing in 1820 AD until the time of his murder in 1844 AD.

6. O'Connor informs us that on another occasion the whole of his work contained in his translation of the 'Chronicles' down to the year 1315 AD were lost in an accidental fire at 'Dangan Castle' in 1809 AD. That one hundred and sixteen pages of the translated pages of the 'Book of Mormon' were lost at one time. In both cases we can see the hand of the adversary in the matter.

7. Both O'Connor and Joseph Smith experienced great persecution and tribulation. However, both were befriended by true and loyal men, who the Lord provided to assist them. One, Sir Francis Burdett of Foremark, standing by O'Connor on more than one occasion, when false charges were made against him by the authorities, and each time attaining his acquittal, and eventually paying for the publishing and printing of the 'Chronicles'! Just as Martin Harris funded the printing of the 'Book of Mormon'. Also just as Joseph Smith was charged on many occasions by the authorities, and placed in prison and being acquitted each time.

8. O'Connor's account of his struggles and misfortunes in attempting to give the world this 'Ancient History' is similar to Joseph Smith's experiences in his attempt to publish the 'Book of Mormon'.

9. O'Connor never completed his work! Unless of course the other Three Volumes of his work do exist somewhere – when in due course they will come forth – be found or be revealed. Just as the sealed portion of the 'Book of Mormon' will be made known.

10. That O'Connor's work was called, and still is called, by some, a forgery. Whereas others claim them to be true records.

    O'Connor and Joseph Smith, both being vilified in Biographical Records, and Publications as deluded – both the 'Chronicles' and the 'Book of Mormon' being referred to as 'the work of their imaginations'. Both men accused of being womanizers, and agitators against the State, etc.

    There are always those who are ready to discredit good men. Always those who are ready to discredit the truth either for selfish or misguided reasons.

11. O'Connor was imprisoned with his brother – just as Joseph Smith was with his.

12. Joseph Smith and O'Connor are similar in physical appearance. The main exception to this 'Strange Parallel' is that it was necessary for Joseph Smith, and his brother, Hyrum, to shed their blood to Seal the Testimony.

    'For where a testament is, there must also of necessity be the death of the testator. For a testament is of force after men are dead. Otherwise it is of no strength at all while the testator liveth.'

    (Hebrews 9: 16-17)

It was also necessary for them to fulfil the Law of Witnesses:- **Matthew 18: 16, John 5: 31, John 8: 17.**

This requirement was due to the fact that the 'Book of Mormon' contains God's Word, and in itself fulfils the Law of Witnesses – the 'Holy Bible' being the other witness. See **2 Nephi 29.**

The 'Chronicles of Eri' are purely an Historical Record, and therefore it was not required that O'Connor should shed his blood as a witness to their validity – but that he suffered much as a witness of his testimony, is in no doubt.

PORTRAIT OF JOSEPH SMITH

The Prophet Joseph Smith from an early newspaper illustration.

Fig. 4: Portrait of Joseph Smith

Chapter Two

The Gaal Sciot of Iber
Family of Noah

Introduction to the Chronicles

The written 'Chronicles of Eri' were commenced by 'EOLUS', who was Chief of Gael-ag from the year 1368 to 1335 BC. He gives the traditionary History of the Scythians from the earliest point of times marked to his own days, until that time passed down from father to son. Eolus acquired his knowledge of writing in Sidon. He ruled over the Gaal Sciot of Iber (known to some Historians as the Milesian Race). This History contains an account of the flood in the days of NOAH, who in the 'Chronicles' is referred to as ARD-FEAR, son of AMLAOC (LAMECH) of the race of AB-SAL or AB-SAIL (Methuselah).

The History also gives an account of the mighty revolution that put an end to the Scythian Dominion in ASIA – and the founding of the Assyrian Empire on the ruins thereof.

Ard-fear is pronounced (AR-FEAR) from which comes our modern 'ARTHUR'. NOAH is the Scythian word for ship (ARK). His descendants being called NAOI-MAID-EIS, NOMADES or NOE'S Multitude.

The 'Chronicles' faithfully record the History of the <u>ERI-AN</u> (ARYAN) peoples. The name Aryan being derived from the Sanskrit word Arya, meaning noble, or 'The Noble Race'. (SANSKRIT is the ancient language of HINDUS in INDIA).

We are informed that the Ark settled at ARARAT (ER-ER-AT) in the area of Southern Russia, known today as ARMENIA (ERI-MEN-IA) meaning, land of the people of ERI.

* See map of Western Asia.

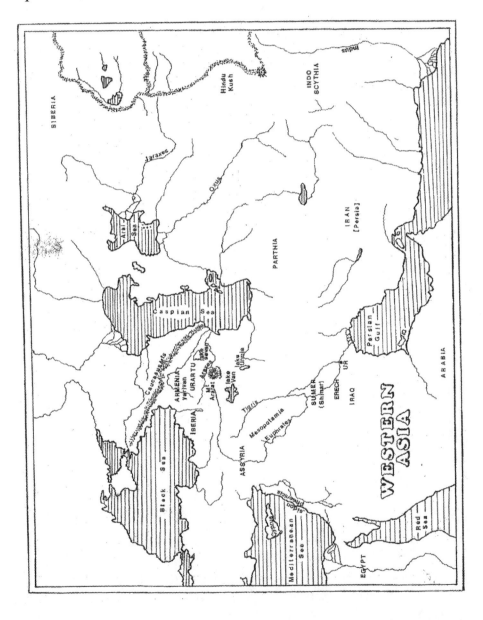

Fig. 5: Map of Western Asia

For some years after the flood the NOAH-MADES or Family of Noah, migrated to various Geographical Areas of the Earth. Japeth's descendants moving North and East into Regions of Russia – Mongolia – China – Japan and a few others into Regions of Asia Minor and Greece, as they are known today.

Ham's descendants migrating South West into Egypt and Africa.

Noah and his son Shem settled in the area North East of the Tigris, on the shores of Lake Van, on the flanks of Mount Ararat, 5,200 feet above sea level, (See Map of Western Asia). Lake Van is about twice the size of Lake Geneva, and was the head water source of both the Tigris and Euphrates.

The Assyrian name for ARARAT or ARMENIA was UR-ARTU (ER-AR-TU) ARMENIA (ERI-MENIA). I-ERI-VAN is the capital city of ARMENIA to this day! The ARAXES (ER-AXES) river was also named accordingly.

On the North Shore of Lake Van, they left a memorial, the settlement of 'ER-CIS'! The name ERIC being a derivative.

After some years, other settlements were established, some moving West towards The Black Sea and into areas of Greece – others moving South following the two big rivers of the Tigris and Euphrates to the Persian Gulf. There they provided the Leadership for the founding of a New Civilization at UR, near the Mouth of the Euphrates, built upon the ruins of another city buried beneath, ten feet of mud deposited on it by the flood.

Others of the same group settled in the Mesopotamian Valley, called in the Bible, The Valley of Shinar or Land between the two rivers. The lower portion of the valley became known as the 'Land of Sumer and Akkad' which later became part of BABYLONIA. The extreme Northern portion became known as 'ASSYRIA' – 'AS-ER-IA'. The Bible refers to Babylonia, in whole, or part, as the 'Land of the Chaldees', and 'Land of Shinar'.

These sons of Shem were known as the 'Mountain People' to others, due to their migration from the high plateaus of ARMENIA to live in UR, which in the Semitic Language means 'Time' and the people as 'Observers of Time'.

Eventually their territory expanded as far as the URAL (ERAL) mountains in the territory of Russia today – and the ARAL (ER-AL) Sea, and into the areas of what is known today as IR-AQ (ER-AQ) and IRAN (ER-AN) ERITREA (ERI-TREA) etc.

The graves of the Kings of UR were uncovered by the British Archaeologist <u>Sir Charles Leonard Wooley</u>, and also a descriptive bit of writing labelled 'LIST OF LARSA No. 1', which reads as follows:- '**Now came the flood. <u>And after the Flood the Kings of the Mountain Peoples assumed dominion</u>**'. It also fell to Wooley to prove the Historical Reality of such a Flood in the 'Land of the Two Rivers'. These '**<u>Kings of the Mountains</u>**' were undoubtedly the Patriarchs of the Bible from Shem to Terah, including (H)eber who was born c. 2378 BC. They were called 'The Children of the KHALDIS' or 'Children of the Rivers', which title (according to Professor L. A. WADDELL) is the source of the names 'CHALDEE' – 'GALATIA' AND 'KELT' or 'CELT'.

At 'UR' they built an Observatory, a High Mound of Stone, flat on top, where they could study the stars by night and measure time thereby. The ruins of the ZIGGURAT were found by C. L. Wooley, who found writings on the site saying that the structure had been begun by URNAMU, and finished by his son DUNGI.

These were the Kings of the 3rd Dynasty of UR (around 2100 BC). It would seem that the great ZIGGURAT of UR had already been built before the birth of Abraham.

As a result of archaeological excavations, conducted by C. L. Wooley, in the years 1922-34 AD, a great deal is known about this City. One building – obviously a College, was uncovered containing a Library of more than 2,000 Volumes. The discovery included Encyclopedias, Dictionaries, Grammars, Reference Books, Annuals, Works of Medicine, Astronomy, Geography, Theology, Law, Civil Government, and Politics. The 'Home of Abraham' has been found, and within it a Library containing Business Documents of his Father, and the 'Family Geneaology' shown previously. His Library was probably the most extensive of any Private Library in the City, for ABRAHAM was a very rich man. '**He was rich in cattle, in silver, and gold**

(GENESIS 23: 2)'. He was one of the wealthiest and most highly educated men of his time.

The Legend and Historical evidence discovered in this Generation, is that it was this Race that built the 'Great Pyramid of Gizeh' in Egypt. Various opinions exist as to who the Builder or Supervisor of that Great Project was.

Some 'experts' tell us that it was IEMHOTEP, who it is claimed was the 'Father of Surveying', and the 'Inventor of Geometry', two sciences that were necessary for the progress of man, and the Expansion of Civilization.

But we have a definite statement concerning the Origin of Astronomy, and Mathematics, given by JOSEPHUS, the Jewish Historian, in his 'Antiquities of the Jews', Book 1 – Chapter 2: 3

> *'They (the Sethites) also were the inventors of that peculiar sort of wisdom which is concerned with the heavenly bodies and their order. And that their inventions might not be lost before they were sufficiently known, upon Adam's prediction that the world was to be destroyed ... they made two pillars ... (one in brick; one in stone) ... they described their discoveries on them both ... to exhibit their discoveries to mankind ... Now this (the pillar of stone) remains in the land of Siriad (Egypt) unto this day'.*

The pillar in the land of Egypt is the 'Great Pyramid of Gizeh'. Egyptian tradition tells us that the architect's name was SISITHRUS or SESORTHOS, which when carefully analysed is a composition of ENOCH and NOAH.

The Chinese Sacred Volume of the 'SHU-KING' also affords confirmation that the Line of ENOCH and NOAH were the originators of the Science of Astronomy. Regarding the FU-HI, who is the Chinese NOAH, the SHU-KING states that he **'constructed astronomical tables, assigned figures (ZODIAC) to the heavenly bodies, and taught the SCIENCE OF THEIR MOTIONS'.**

'The Book of Jubilees' is one of non-canonical books of the Bible, yet it <u>contains valuable information concerning the first 2500 years of Adamic History, ending about the time of the Exodus from Egypt</u>. In its Fourth Chapter we read of Enoch or Hanok.

> *'He was the first one among the children of men that are born on the earth to learn writing and knowledge and wisdom. And he wrote 'The Signs of Heaven', according to the order of their months in a book, that the sons of men might know the time of year according to their separate months. He was the first to write a testimony, and he testified to the children of men concerning the generations of the earth, and explained the weeks of the jubilees, and made known to them the days of the years, and arranged the months and explained the Sabbaths of the years, as we made them known to him. And what was and what will be he saw in a vision of the night in a dream, and as it will happen to the children of men in their generations until the day of judgement, he saw and learned everything and wrote it as a testimony and laid that testimony on the earth over all the children of men and for their generations'.*

(Book of Jubilees: pp 16)

These statements from JOSEPHUS and others from the SHU-KING and BOOK OF JUBILEES, inform us the science of Astronomy – Geometry – Surveying and many other skills were known to NOAH – even ENOCH, the 7th Patriarch from ADAM, son of JARED and father of METHUSELAH long before the flood!

That it was ENOCH who built the Great Pyramid of Gizeh standing to this day in Egypt.

That the Gizeh Pyramid was not a burial tomb, but that it was a great observatory, and its peculiar passage system is said to contain a message of the World's History and Plan of Salvation – a Literal Witness in Stone.

That the pyramid is a Witness of the Ancient's Understanding of the Sciences of Astronomy – Geometry – and the Earth and its Planetary Systems. Anyone making a study of the Great Pyramid will realise how advanced these Ancients were in these Sciences.

We are also informed in the 'BOOK OF ABRAHAM' in the 'PEARL OF GREAT PRICE' that Abraham was **skilled in these sciences.** (ABRAHAM – CHAPTER 3).

JOB mentions the Monument:- JOB   18: 4;
                                   38: 1-4

As also does ISAIAH:- ISA. 19: 19-20

JOB was descended from the line of SHEM – he also had a great knowledge of Astronomy and Geometry:- JOB   9: 9
                                   18: 4
                                   26: 7,13
                                   37: 22
                                   <u>38: 1-4, 31-32</u>
                                   41: 1

'UR' – The Symbol of Fire

According to Young's Analytical Concordance of the Holy Bible (Robert Young LL.D) 'UR' means Light – Brightness. 'URI' means Enlightened. 'URIM' means Lights – or according to other authorities including Dr. Roger O'Connor – 'URIM and THUMMIM' means 'The perfection of fire and heat'.

'UR' – The Symbol of Time

In approaching this subject it is well if I remind the readers that in the original Hebrew there are no vowels as in the English A.E.I.O.U. In Hebrew the vowel sound being made in the pronunciation, therefore, the word <u>UR</u> could be pronounced AR, ER, IR, OR, UR. Also the letter 'H' was silent. For example the Hebrew word for Covenant – 'BRITH', would be spelt 'BRT' as also the name DAN would be spelt 'DN' of which various words can be formed using the sounds of the five vowels, i.e. DAN, DEN, DIN, DON, DUN and BARAT, BARET, BARIT, BAROT, BARUT, and many other combinations.

In the <u>Book of Judges: Chapter Twelve</u> we have evidence also of the inability of the Ephraimites to sound their 'H's. The Gileadites had been successful in the battle, there were many refugees using the 'passages of the Jordan' river. The Gileadites were seeking out the Ephraimites by making them pronounce the word 'SHIBBOLETH', and we find that they could not frame to pronounce it right, for they said 'SIBBOLETH'. In a similar manner that many Englishmen today do not sound their 'H's or able to pronounce the 'TH' together, saying Fa'<u>v</u>'er for Father, Mo'<u>v</u>'er for Mother, '<u>T</u>'ousands for Thousands, Some'<u>f</u>'ink for Something, Toge'<u>v</u>'er for Together, etc. This trait is more evident with Cockney Londoners, in Liverpool, Yorkshire and some areas of Scotland.

The German word 'UHR' means 'TIME' or 'TIMEPIECE'.

In French time is 'HE-UR-E'.

In English we say 'HO-UR'.

We find it in the word 'TA-UR-US' or TAURUS.

Therefore, when Abraham was called out of UR by God, he was destined to open a new age, or new time period in the Sign of the Constellation of the BULL, or the TA-UR-US (UR-US) age. (GENESIS 12).

The first fulfilment of the Lord's Covenant with Abraham was that Abraham became the Father of ISAAC, the son of promise in whose name Abraham's seed was to be called, namely 'SAXONS' or 'ISAAC'S-SONS' by his legal wife, SARAH. In this calling out of TIME (UR), he and his seed became a 'servant people' under covenant, or contract, with God.

We also find the word 'UR' in the name of ABRAHAM'S third wife KET-UR-AH, by her ABRAHAM had six sons which became the progenitors of the INDIAN ('URDU' – 'ERDU') peoples. Here Abraham's progeny retained the memory of their Sire by calling themselves (A)BRAHIMS – AB-RA-MINS, also giving honour to their origin by holding sacred the BULL, or URUS, calling them BRAMAH cattle.

We also find the word 'UR' in CH-UR-CH. Jesus said **'I am ALPHA and OMEGA' (beginning and the end).**

The Greek letters for Christ are CH or X (CHI). So in the very word 'CH-UR-CH' we see CHRIST (CH) first, then UR (in time), and CH (CHRIST) at the end – THE CHURCH IN TIME, CH – CHI is pronounced KEE.

The founding of his CHURCH IN TIME was begun in UR with the calling out of Abraham, and we now await the end of the Church age at Christ's soon return when 'TIME' will be no more.

The Scottish word 'KIRK' is derived from CHI-UR-CHI pronounced 'KIRK' KI-UR-KI.

The significance of this is that ALPHA and OMEGA are the first and last letters of the Greek Alphabet in which the New Testament was written, and by using them as a name for himself our Lord is declaring that he is God – The First and Last.

Further we should note that the words ALPHA and OMEGA in the Scripture quotations REV 1: 11; 21: 6; 22: 13 begin with Capital Letters. They are, therefore, proper nouns, and used together constitute a name.

From this emerges the fact that the first and last letters of the Greek Alphabet, when used together, form the monogram, or name of God.

This also applies to the Hebrew of the Old Testament.

ISAIAH 44: 6; 48: 12

The first and last letters of the Hebrew Alphabet are ALEPH and TAU. And modern research is moving rapidly towards a recognition that in the original Hebrew (The Noahic or Enochian) Alphabet they were written **X** and **+**

This is amazing, for when they are put together to form the name of God – that name appears as a crossed cross – which is a symbol of the 'UNION JACK', the British United Kingdom Flag – and the only Flag to bear such symbols!

The City of J-ER-USALEM

J-ER-USALEM had a long history prior to the advent of the ISRAELITES but it did not always bear this familiar name. Remotely, it was known as <u>URIEL</u> or <u>ARIEL</u> or Altar of God (ALT-ER) = UR-I-EL (ISAIAH 29: 1-4). Names showing that the original inhabitants were SHEMITES. Melchizedec himself being the Ancient Patriarch SHEM himself. (BOOK OF JASHER p45: 11).

Judea or Palestine, as it became known was part of the inheritance given to Abraham and his seed. This area was part of the lands allocated to them when the Earth was divided (apportioned) out by the Lord. (DEUT. 32: 7-9).

The Egyptians referred to the city as HAR-EL.

In ABRAHAMS day it had become SALEM.

At a later date it is referred to as URU-SALEM in the Tell el Armana Letters, retaining the archaic word 'UR', which means city, and sometimes Capital City.

CHAPTER THREE

Early Britons
The First Settlers

Part of the Shemites were prevented by the Assyrians from migrating South down the Mesopotamian Valley. This group returned to ARMENIA. However, instead of settling with their kinsmen, the Gaal Sciot of Iber – they continued their Westward trek <u>(about 1800 BC)</u> crossing the Caucasus Mountains into Europe under the Leadership of HU-GADARN HYSICION (ISAACSON) – known in the Kymric as 'HU the MIGHTY'.

This was probably the first migration of the SCIOT of IBER known as the SCYTH-IAN people – (SCIOT-IAN) – (SCYT-IAN) – (SCOTTISH) to other Nations. This group entered into the British Isles and formed the early Welsh – (Silurian) and Scottish Nations.

WALES – being a derivative of GAELS – (KYMRY)

SCOTS – being a derivative from SCIOT – (CELTS)

From Keltic Lore it appears that HU-GADARN the Mighty was the Leader of the First Colony of the KYMRY into Britain about the time of Abraham. In the 'Historic Triads of the Island of Britain' – (Ancient Celtic Literature) – he is described as one of the 'Three Benefactors of the Race of the KYMRY', one of the 'Three Primary Sages of his Adopted Land', one of the 'Three Pillars of the Race of the Island of Britain'. He is reputed to have established 'Patriarchal Worship' wherever he went. He was regarded as the personification of intellect and culture, rather than of physical strength, as in Greece. As a peacemaker he stands paramount, for he promoted agriculture, and it is said of him that he would not have lands by forfeiture and contention, but **'of equity and peace'.**

In Welsh Archaeology, Hu-Gadarn is commemorated for **'having made poetry the vehicle of memory and record'**, and to have been the inventor of the Triads. To him also is attributed the introduction of several arts, such as glass making, and writing in OGAM characters. Hu-Gadarn is also credited for building the great stone circle (Observatory) at Stonehenge and <u>Avebury</u>, called AB-IRI in the Hebrew (AB-ERI). Much has been written about these Ancient Stone Circles and Mounds.

The question may be asked – What prompted the Gaals of Sciot of Iber to migrate to these Islands of Britain? The answer is found in the Triads.

In the Ancient Literature concerning the primitive migrations of the KYMRY is one of the oldest recorded traditions of the flood:-

> *'Long before the **Kymry** came into Britain the **Llyn Llion**, or Great Deep (literally the abyss of waters), broke up and inundated the whole earth.*
>
> *The Island, afterwards known as Britain, shared the general catastrophe. One vessel floated over the waters, this was the ship of **Newydd Nav Neivion.** In it were two individuals preserved – **Dwy Van** (the man of God) and **Dwy Vach** (the woman of God). By the posterity of these two the earth gradually re-peopled.*
>
> **The ship of Newydd Nav Neivion was built in Britain, and was one of its three mighty works.**
>
> *For a long time after the subsiding of the deluge the Kymry dwelt in the Summer Land, between the **Sea of Afez** and **Deffrobani.** The land being exposed to sea floods, they resolved, under the guidance of **Hu Gadarn** to seek again the White Island of the West, where their father <u>**Dwy Van**</u>, had built the ship of Newydd Nav Neivion.*
>
> **They journeyed westward towards the setting sun,** *being many in number and men of great heart and strength (**Cedeirn**, mighty*

ones, giants). They came in sight of the Alps, and then **part of their migration diverged southward – these are the Kymry (Umbri) of Italy.** *The others, consisting of the three tribes of the Kymry,* **the Brython and the Lloegrwys,** *crossed the Alps. Along either side of the Alps, near the sea, part of the* **Lloegrwys settled; these are the Ligurains of Italy and Gaul.**

Pursuing their course still further they crossed the River of Eddies, the Slow River, the Rough River, the Bright River (the Rhone, the Arar, **the Garonne,** *the Loire), till they reached* **Gwasgwyn** *(Gascony, the Vine-land). Thence they turned northward and part of the Brython settled in a land they named* **Llydaw ar y Mor Ucha** *(the land or expansion on the Upper Sea* **Armorica).** **The Kymry still held onward until they saw the cliffs of the White Island.** *Then they built ships and in them passed over the Hazy Ocean (* **Mor Tawch)** *and took possession of the Island. And they found no living creature on it but* **bisons, elks, bears, beavers and water monsters.** *And they took possession of it not by war, nor by conquest, not by oppression, but by right of man over nature. And they sent to the* **Brythons in Llydaw, and to the Lloegrwys on the Continent,** <u>**and to as many as came they gave the East and the North of the Island. And the Kymry dwelt in the West.**</u>

These three Tribes were of one race, origin and speech. These are the three Pacific Tribes of the Isle of Britain, because they came in mutual good-will, peace and love; **and over them reigned Hu the Mighty, the one rightful Sovereign of the Island. And they called the Island the White Island (Ynys Wen),** *and the Island of the mighty ones. Its name Britain, or Prydain, was not yet known'.*

This account is a very striking one. The date precedes, by many centuries, the earliest traditions of Greece and Rome. Its statements are in entire accordance with the results of the most recent investigations into the origin of Language and Nations.

It reveals that the 'Ark' (ship of Newydd Nav Neivion) was built in the islands we know today as Britain! These facts being correct then we must accept that Noah and his family lived here also!

Yes truth is stranger than fiction.

All the most Ancient Writers of Greece and Rome concur in stating that the KYMRY or GOMERIDOE, were under appellations slightly varied, the Primo-genital or Oldest Family in the World. Along their first habitation, the shores of the Euxine and the Sea of Azov, they were known as KIMRY or KIMMEROI, the peninsula which formed part of their dominions retains their name KIMRIA, corrupted into CRIMEA. South of the CAUCASIAN Range of Mountains, they were called GOMRAI and SCYTHS. As stated earlier the most important positions in that area retain their primitive Kymric names GUMRE (Chief Fortress) VAN (the peak) ERIVAN (the peaks on which the ERI settled).

The reason therefore for this expedition, led by HU-GADARN was to once again locate the 'White Island of the West', where their father, Dwy 'VAN' had built the Ship of Newydd-<u>Nav</u>-Neivion ('Nav becoming VAN in reverse).

We are also informed that a group detached themselves at the Alps, diverted South and formed the KYMRY (UMBRI) people of Italy. The others consisting of three tribes KYMRY, BRYTHON and LLOEGRWYS crossed the Alps. The Lloegrwys settling on the Mediterranean Coast of France, Northern Italy and Switzerland.

The Brythons settled in ARMORICA (AM-ERI-CA?) which forms part of Brittany in Western France and the Basque territory of Northern Spain – establishing the BRETON and BASQUE communities around the Pyrenees, and those in the area of what is called Normandy.

The KYMRY pursued their original quest – eventually crossing the channel and settling in the British Isles from whence their forefathers had come.

According to these records the island was uninhabited except for numerous and varied animals including BISONS, ELKS, BEARS, BEAVERS and WATER MONSTERS!

We are informed that the Kymry sent to the Brythons and Lloegrwys on the Continent inviting them to join them in the Island of their Fathers – and as many as came they gave the EAST and NORTH (East Anglia, Kent, Essex and part of the South East) – (Northumbria and Scotland), whereas the KYMRY dwelt in the WEST (Wales, C-Umbria, Devon, Somerset, Wiltshire, etc.). And over them reigned 'HU the Mighty', the 'One Rightful Sovereign of the Island'.

Now for anyone to suggest that Noah and his family dwelt in these Islands and to further suggest that the Ark was built here usually results in a 'knee-jerk response' accompanied by loud laughter, and would raise a question as to one's mental health, with the thought of sending for the men in white coats! Nevertheless, until it is proven differently, the account given in these Ancient Records is just as valid as any other, even more valid.

Certainly truth is stranger than fiction!

It must also be remembered that the Life and Times of HU-GADARN were contemporary with that of ABRAHAM, and we know that the Ancient Patriarch, SHEM, was still living at that time, and he, being one of Noah's sons must have passed on to his posterity a '<u>first hand account</u>' of the events of the flood. <u>At what location of the Earth he had lived with his family</u>, and of the events surrounding the building of the Ark, surely that is a reasonable conclusion.

The Bible also informs us that the Ancient Patriarchs from Adam had a knowledge of Divine Laws. In GENESIS 26 we are informed that ISAAC was to receive both temporal and spiritual blessings.

> *'Because that Abraham obeyed my voice, and kept my charge, my commandments, my statutes, and my laws.'*

> (GENESIS 26: 5)

Even Noah long before Abraham had the Laws of God. He knew which animals were 'clean' and those which were 'not clean' – GENESIS 7: 1-2. He was also commanded to impose Capital Punishment on those who committed pre-meditated murder.

> *'Whoso sheddeth man's blood by man shall his blood be shed:*
> *for in the image of God made he man.'*

(GENESIS 9: 1-6)

The building of the ARK was no mean feat either. We are informed its dimensions were:-   300 cubits in length
50 cubits in width
30 cubits in height

(GENESIS 6: 13-16)

A cubit is accepted as being anything between 21" to 24". In that case the approximate size of the Ark was:-   500 ft in length
83 ft in width
50 ft in height

With three separate decks. Just as big, if not bigger than a modern Liner of today!

Contrary to the usual understanding that it took NOAH one hundred and twenty years to complete, the 'BOOK OF JASHER' informs us that the task was completed in five years.

> *'In his five hundred and ninety fifth year Noah commenced to make*
> *the Ark, and he made the Ark in five years, as the Lord commanded!*

(JASHER 5: 34)

Proving that the Ancients had all the skills and technology, as we have today.

The Science of Dowsing

Moreover, HERODUTUS the famous Greek Historian of the Fifth Century BC in the Sixty Seventh Chapter of his work, informs us that this great Scythian People were noted for their mode of divination 'BY TWIGS' – that is, in the Art of Dowsing, an almost forgotten Science – Yes! I do call it a Science, because it has proved to be so on many occasions, when our so-called Modern Technology has failed. This Science was known to the Ancient Biblical Patriarchs from Adam to Moses. Divination by rods, sticks, pendulums etc. is an art peculiar to the Anglo Saxon Celtic people to this day.

National Traditions and Druidism

National traditions maintain that the Scythian Kymry possessed from the earliest period of their existence a knowledge of the true God, and embodied it into their theological code as one of the fundamental doctrines of Druidism.

In studying the primeval religion of Britain we should never lose sight of the fact that the Universe or Zodiac was the Bible of the Ancients. In it was revealed the whole Plan of Salvation.

> *'The heavens declare the glory of God, and the firmament sheweth his handywork'.*

(Psalm 19)

So wrote King David:-

> *'And God said, Let there be 'lights' in the firmament of heaven to divide the day from the night, AND LET THEM BE FOR 'SIGNS', and for seasons, and for days, and years.*

(GENESIS 1: 14)

The wonders of nature were to them as 'the voice of the ALL-Father', directing their lives and unfolding to their reverent observation the intimations of the stupendous circle of the Universal Law on which our Earth revolves with Sun and Stars in the service of a Supreme God. By the movements of the Heavenly Bodies they ordered their lives, regulated the Times and the Seasons, the Days and the Years, fixed Religious Festivals and all Agricultural Proceedings.

This sublime Study of the '<u>MANUSCRIPTS OF GOD</u>' brought man into direct intercourse with the highest mind and intelligence. One of the Greatest Testimonies to the Spiritual Character of the Religion of our Forefathers is the fact that no Graven Image or Inscribed Stone of any kind has ever been discovered of Pre-Roman origin in Great Britain! Not that the primitive religion is unrepresented, for numerous incense-burners of clay have been found in the vicinity of the STONE CIRCLES which witness the common use of the Divine Ordinance of Burning Incense (symbolic of prayer) in the Druidic Religion as in the Patriarchal Worship of the Israelites. Also in the Gold Room of the British Museum are to be seen several beautiful examples of gold crescent-shaped breast plates, similar to those worn by Aaron.

At a meeting of the British Association 1836, held at Stonehenge, when Geology was in its infancy, it was discovered that the Altar-Stone was of 'Fire-Stone', pointing to the possibility that here, as in the Outer Court of the Tabernacle in the Wilderness, may have been an Altar of Burnt Incense. Many references are made in the old Welsh Writings of the **'Sacred Fire'**! **'Not mean was the place appointed for conference before the <u>Perpetual Fire</u>'** – may be descriptive of Stonehenge:- the beautiful poem of 'The Chair of Taliesin' commences, **'<u>I am he who keeps up the fire</u>'.**

HU-GADARN and his successor Aedd Mawr founded DRUIDISM which they divided into three orders – DRUIDS, BARDS, OVATES – and allotted to them different offices and duties in Business and State, Druid being the highest office.

The title DRUID, in Welsh 'der wydd' is a compound of 'dar', superior, and 'gwydd', priest – High Priesthood. The order numbered thirty one chief seats of education similar to our Great Universities today.

Caesar states the headquarters of the Druids were in Britain, and that those who aspired to be initiated in the more profound mysteries came to the British Islands for instruction.

They were instructed in all aspects of learning. Their training covered a twenty year period. No one was admissible to the Order who could not prove his Genealogy, from free parents for nine generations back. This restriction placed the Order almost entirely in the hands of the aristocracy, making it literally a 'Royal Priesthood'.

The examinations preparatory to full initiation into the highest grades of BARD and DRUID was very severe. Each candidate had to pass three examinations, three successive years, before the Druidic College on subjects of Natural Philosophy, Astronomy, Mathematics, Geometry, Medicine, Theology, Civil Laws and many more. Nothing was written, all had to be committed to memory.

Their motto was:- **'Y gwir er byn y Byd' – 'The Truth Against the World'** – it survives to the present day.

The Druidic Trinity consisted of BELI, TARAN, ESU or YESU. When Christianity preached Jesus as God, it preached the most familiar name of its own deity to Druidism. To this day the Ancient KYMRIC tongue continues to use the Druidic 'YESU'.

The Ancient 'Magi'

The Latin equivalent for 'DRUID' is 'MAGI'! Could it be that the MAGI of the New Testament story were of British origin? <u>Tradition always bears a vein of truth however fantastic it may seem.</u>

Those to whom the Almighty chose to reveal what the heavens have to say to man were the descendants of Shem.

The Scythian Kelts were their direct descendants, they were further advanced in the subject of Astronomy than any other people. This knowledge was a major part of Druidic training.

They called their new home **NEW SUMER-LAND** as opposed to their OLD SUMER-LAND in Mesopotamia – today it has been Anglicised to **SOMERSET!**

I believe the Druidic Magi knew of the prophecy given by MICAH (Chapter 5: 2). They also knew of the prophecy by a man named ZOHAR who wrote a scroll which many years later was going to be translated and printed. When the document was being examined it was ascertained that part of it was missing, but, in what was left was a prophecy which, when translated read, **'WHEN THE MESSIAH IS BORN, A BRILLIANT STAR WILL RISE IN THE EAST'.** ZOHAR was a one-time chief of the Hittites, of the City of Mamre, he was a descendant of HETH. He is mentioned in GENESIS 23: 8 and 25: 9.

The account of the visit of the MAGI is found in MATTHEW 2, here we are informed that the 'Wise Men' 'saw his star in the East'. For a star to be seen in the East one must be located geographically West of Judea!

Although we are informed in Verse Two that, 'there came wise men from the East to Jerusalem', does it, of necessity mean that they resided in a land East of Jerusalem? Their approach into Jerusalem could have been through the East Gate of the City – could it not?

Another point is – if they lived in a land somewhere East of Palestine – Why did it take them almost two years to arrive? For we are informed that Jesus was by that time 'a child'. And after the departure of the 'Wise Men' the infamous King Herod ordered the murder of all the children that were in Bethlehem, and in all the coasts thereof, from two years old and under, according to the time which he had diligently enquired of the wise men (Verse 16). Throughout this account Jesus is referred to as 'a young child' – not a baby.

This incident may have been the 'spur' which caused the ready acceptance of Christianity in all parts of these Western Isles – established by the Saviour's Great Uncle Joseph of ARIMATHEA (ERI-MATHEA) about 38 AD!

The so-called 'tradition' or 'Myth' of Joseph of Arimathea's connection with Britain has been called to question many times by 'so-called' Historians always ready to reject a truth or fact. There is so much Documentary Proof existing of the Saviour's Great Uncle being involved in Commercial Mining Operations in Britain that it is no longer a tradition. Documentary evidence in the Ancient British Chronicles, the Domesday Book, and many others, that if these so-called Critics and Historians would take time to investigate, they would have to accept the overwhelming evidence which they reveal regarding Joseph of Arimathea's connections in Britain. But we do not have to rely upon British History or Historical Records to prove this fact.

Roman Catholic Historian Testifies

CARDINAL BARONIUS is considered to be the most outstanding Historian of the Roman Catholic Church. He was curator of the Vatican Library, a man of learning and a reliable and facile writer.

Quoting from his 'ECCLESIASTICAL ANNALA', which refers to the exodus from Jerusalem 36 AD, the mystery is solved as to the fate of Joseph of Arimathea and others who went into exile shortly after the death of the Saviour.

He writes:-

> *'In that year (36 AD) the party mentioned was exposed to the sea in a vessel without sails or oars. The vessel drifted finally to Marseilles and they were saved. From Marseilles Joseph and his company passed into Britain, and after preaching the Gospel there died.'*

This statement is supported by reliable Greek and Roman Authorities including affirmation in the 'Jewish Encyclopaedia' under 'ARLES'.

Cardinal Baronius in his Great Work, quoted from MISTRAL, in 'MIREO' and another Ancient Document in the Vatican Library. He names them one by one.

Here is a list of the occupants of that vessel:-

MARY wife of Cleopas
MARTHA   MARY MAGDALENE
LAZARUS   MARCELLA, the Bethany sister's maid
EUTROPIUS   MAXIMIN
SALOME   MARTIAL
CLEAN   TROPHIMUS
SATURNIUS   SIDONIUS (Restitutus)
JOSEPH OF ARIMATHEA

No doubt this will come as a surprise to many Christians for it shows that Christianity was brought to Britain by Joseph of Arimathea the Great Uncle to Jesus – (he being a brother to the Virgin Mary's Father).

Many other writers insist that there was another member to this party not recorded in the 'MISTRAL' report. Mary, the Mother of Jesus, along with tradition, a great deal of extant documentary testimony substantiates the presence of Mary being with Joseph, he having been appointed by the Apostle John as 'Paranymphos' (guardian) to the Virgin Mary due to the fact that he was her uncle.

Joseph of Arimathea was a 'Billionaire' in his day. The Scriptures classify him a 'Rich Man'. His wealth came from his Mining interests in Devon and Cornwall where he owned both Tin and Lead Mines.

The tradition is that on the occasional visits he made to Britain to oversee those interests he brought with him his Great Nephew Jesus, the son of Mary.

The great mystery in the life of the Saviour is that there is no recorded History written, even by the Gospel Writers of the events of his life from the age of twelve unto the time of his appearance in Judea at the age of thirty when he presented himself to his cousin John (Baptist) to be baptised, even John did not recognize him at the time! And families were very close in those days!

In fact, upon the Saviour's arrival 'back home' he was made to pay 'strangers' tax! (MATT 17: 24-27), so where had he been for those eighteen years? Could it be that the Saviour received his formal education during this period in the Great Druidical Colleges of Britain?

The Saviour would be readily accepted in the Druidical Institutions due to the friendship which existed between Joseph of Arimathea and the Druidic Priesthood, and secondly, and just as importantly, the Saviour could quite easily show evidence of his 'Royal' Genealogy from 'free' Parents for more than nine generations.

This seems so fantastic as to be almost unbelievable.

But:-

> *'There (really) are more things in heaven and earth, Horatio,*
>
> *Than are dreamt of in your philosophy...'*

Shakespeare, <u>Hamlet</u> Act 1, Sc. 5

<u>The Druids and Christianity</u>

Upon the introduction of Christianity into Britain about 36 AD, the Druids were called upon, not so much to reverse their Ancient Faith, <u>as to lay it down for a more fuller and perfect revelation</u>. No country can show a more rapid natural merging of native religion into Christianity than that which was witnessed in Britain in the First Century AD. The readiness with which the Druids accepted Christianity, turning their facilities, colleges, and places of worship to Christian uses are facts which the Modern Historian has overlooked or ignored.

The Druidical teaching concerning Man's spiritual nature is comprised in the following Triad:-

> In every person there is a soul,
> In every soul there is intelligence,

In every intelligence there is a thought,
In every thought there is either good or evil,
In every evil there is death,
In every good there is life,
In every life there is God.

The Druidical Symbol of the name of Deity are Three Rods or Pencils of Light – symbolizing the Trinity of Father, Son and Holy Spirit.

The Sacred Symbol of the British Gorsedd, the Three Rays or Rods, survive in two forms, in the 'Three Feathers' of the Prince of Wales, and in the 'Broad Arrow' of the Government. When Edward III re-founded on the Windsor Table Mound the British King Arthur's 'Order of the Round Table' as a reward for those Knights who had won for him his victories in France, he adopted the Gorsedd Symbol, the sign of Spiritual and Temporal Power of the Ancient Keltic Kings and Priests, as the cognizance of his son, the Black Prince. In the form of Three Ostrich Feathers, the Three Golden Rays have been borne from that time by successive Princes of Wales.

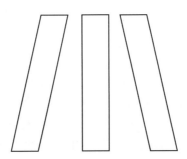

'DUW A DIGON'

(GOD AND ENOUGH)

Those readers who desire to visualise a Druidic Assembly, could do no better than be present at one of the National Gorsedds in Wales. The locality is chosen always at the Eisteddfod of the previous year – usually a meadow large enough to accommodate thousands of people who assemble to take part in these popular, purely Educational Contests, as they now are.

A circle is formed of Twelve Un-hewn Stones, symbolic of the Signs of the Zodiac (and similar to those erected by Moses at Sinai, and Joshua and others at a later time). In the centre is the Large Maen Llog or Logan Stone, symbolic of the '<u>Rock</u>' which is Christ. Druidism itself was ordinarily known as 'Y Maen' – the stone.

The Maen Llog is placed in the central position of the circle and must be untouched by any tool. It is supposed to have the same symbolic significance as the Sacred Rock on Mount Moriah that rises from the rocky platform of Mount Zion, the Mount of the Stone has been regarded from the time of King David and Solomon as the most Sacred Ground in Jerusalem.

The stone is still on the original site – which today is in possession of a Muslim Temple – The Dome of the Rock.

Twelve Bards, one by each stone, guard the Gorsedd Circle today as in times past, and two 'Keepers of the Gate' are stationed at the entrance, which is on the East side. The ground plan of the Circle is similar to that of Stonehenge. At the entrance of the Circle may be seen Three Prostrate Un-hewn Stones pointing outwards from the central 'Maen Llogan', these represent the Ancient Kymric Symbol of the Awen, or Holy Wings, the Three Rays or Rods of Light signifying the Eye of Light, or the Radiating Light of Divine Intelligence shed upon the Druidic Circle.

It is the Sacred Symbol that proclaims from generation to generation the National Faith in the Eternal Shadowing of the Divine Wings.

In the earliest days every Druid wore the Symbol of the Ineffable Name of Deity, in Gold Rays on the front of his <u>Linen Mitre</u>.

Like the High Priest of old he is clad in white and wears a gold crested, shaped breast plate. He wears a crown of bronze oak leaves around the LINEN CAP upon his head.

When all have taken up their respective positions within the circle, four long blasts on a Silver Trumpet announce the fact to the vast concourse.

The Arch-Druid, with uplifted outstretched arms then proceeds to open the congress with the Gorsedd Prayer, reputed to be as old as 'The Institution'.

The Gorsedd Prayer

GWEDDI'R ORSEDD (The Gorsedd Prayer)

> Dyro Dduw dy Nawdd;
>
> Ag yn Nawd, Nerth;
>
> Ag yn Nerth, Deall;
>
> Ag yn Neall, Gwybod;
>
> Ag yngwybod, Gwybod y Cyfiawn;
>
> Ag yngwybod y Cyfiawn, ei Garu;
>
> Ag o Garu, Caru pob Hanfod;
>
> Ag ymhob Hanfod, Caru Duw;
>
>> Duw a phob Daioni

Translation

> Grant, O God, Thy Protection
>
> And in Protection, Strength
>
> And in Strength, Understanding
>
> And in Understanding, Knowledge
>
> And in Knowledge, the Knowledge of Justice
>
> And in Knowledge of Justice, the Love of it

And in that Love, the Love of all Existences

And in the Love of all Existences, the Love of God

God and all Goodness.

Other Druidic Doctrines taught that:-

The Three Primary Principals of Wisdom were:-

Wisdom to the Laws of God

Concern for the Welfare of Mankind, and

Suffering with Fortitude all the Accidents of Life.

There are three ways of searching the heart of Man:-

In the thing he is not aware of

In the manner he is not aware of

And at the time he is not aware of.

There are three men that all ought to look upon with affection:-

He that, with affection, looks at the face of the earth

That is delighted with rational works of art, and

That looks lovingly on little infants.

And further:-

The things called rewards or punishments are so secured by eternal ordinances that they are not consequences, but properties of our acts and habits. Except for crimes against society, the measure of punishment should be that which nature itself deals to the delinquent.

'Perfect penitence is entitled to pardon. That penitence is perfect, which makes the utmost compensation in its power for wrong inflicted, and willingly submits to the penalty prescribed. <u>The atonements of penitents, who voluntarily submit themselves to death in expiation of guilt incurred, is perfect. The souls of all such pass on to the higher cycles of existence'. 'The justice of God cannot be satisfied except by the sacrifice of life in lieu of life'</u> (Blood Atonement). 'Matter is the creation of God. Without God it cannot exist. Nature is the action of God through the medium of matter'. 'The Universe is matter as ordered and systematized by the intelligence of God. It was created by God's pronouncing His own name – at the sound of which light and the heavens sprang into existence. The name of God is itself a creative power. What in itself that name is, is known to God only. All music or natural melody is a faint and broken echo of the creative name'.

'There are Three Primeval Unities, and more than one of each cannot exist, One God, One Truth and One Point of Liberty, where all opposites preponderate'.

Three things proceed from the Three Primeval Unities:-

All of Life – All that is Good – and All Power.

'God consists necessarily of Three things:- The Greatest of Life – The Greatest of Knowledge – and the Greatest of Power, and what is the Greatest, there can be no more than one of anything'.

<u>Laws Pertaining to the Druidic Priesthood</u>

The Three Ultimate intentions of Bardism:- to Reform Morals and Customs, to Secure Peace, and to celebrate the Praise of all that is Good and Excellent.

Three Things are forbidden to the Bard:- Immorality, to Satirize, and to Bear Arms.

The Three Joys of the Bards of Britain:- the Increase of Knowledge, the Reformation of Manners, and the Triumphs of Peace over the Lawless and Depredators.

These 'Things' and 'Laws' seem very familiar to Bible Students.

These 'Things' have been mentioned here to once and for all eliminate the false impressions that are given to us by some 'so-called' Historians in their remarks about the 'painted savages of Britain' and the human sacrifices of their Druidic Priesthood.

The Pillars of Fire

The Large and Sacred Mounds, or Gorsedds, entered into the Domestic as well as the Religious lives of our Forefathers. We learn from a 'Custom of the Beltan', or 'Spring Festival', when 'Sacred Fire' was brought down by means of a most Powerful Reflecting Mirror of Metal called 'Drych Haul Kibddar', this filled the Stone Circles with a Blaze of Glory. The same procedure being enacted at the 'Summer Solstice', or 'White-sin-tide' or 'Whitsun' – and the 'Mid Winter Festival' when the Mistletoe was cut with the Golden Crescent from the Sacred Oak, and became known as 'Christmas'.

No City in the World ever presented a more majestic appearance than did the Kymric Porth of Llandin, or London, on the occasion of these Great Solistal Festivals, when the 'Fires of God' blazed upon the summits of the four Sacred Mounds, the Open Air Sanctuaries of our Forefathers, roofed by the heavens, and floored by the bare earth. We may conjure up the scene, where the watery stretches of the river reflected in molten gold the 'Pillars of Fire', symbolizing the presence of God!

The Accompanying Diagram, based on the Ordinance Map shows the relative position of these Pre-Historic Mounds.

About four miles North West of St. Pauls towered the largest and most important, The Llandin (Llan = sacred, din = eminence, in Welsh signifying a High Place of Worship), Parliament Hill, 322 feet high. About three miles South East and second in height and size, came the Penton (Pen = head, ton

= sacred mound), never known, even at the present day, by other than its Keltic title.

'Piled up' on the foreshore of the Thames were two entirely Artificial Mounds, the Bryn Gwyn, and the <u>Tothill</u>. On the Bryn Gwyn (Bryn = hill, Gwyn = white or holy), the White Mount, now stands the White Tower of the Tower of London. Two miles West, on Thorn-ey Island, was the Tothill (Tot = Sacred Mound). Not a vestige of the pre-historic Mound of the Tothill is now to be seen, but the memory of this Ancient 'Place of Assembly' survives in the names of Tothill Street and Tothill Fields. (Thorney = Isle of Thorns)

By the Welsh, these 'High Places of Worship' are called Gorsedds, a compound of two words, namely 'Gor' signifying 'Superior', 'Uttermost' or 'Supreme', and 'Sedd' (dd pronounced 'th' as in them), 'Seat'. <u>Therefore Gorsedd means 'Supreme Seat'</u> and the name is used by the Welsh Britons for the Throne of the Monarch to this day.

London, as the city is called today, is a derivative of the Cymric word 'Llandin' = High – Eminent Place of Worship.

The Scythian Gaels of 'Wales' (and Wales is only a derivative of GAELS) were known as SILURES by the Romans. The word SILURES is derived from the Scythian word 'SUL-UR-EIS', which means 'the Tribe of the Sun and Fire'. As I have pointed out previously in the 'Exposition', these tribes were not Sun or Fire worshippers, but these represented the 'personification' of the invisible God.

The Twelve Tribes of Israel were also of this same Scythian Ancestry, they were also the Tribe of the 'Sun and Fire', recognizing in these physical elements the personification of God. If you doubt this, or it seems unbelievable, let me ask you this question. When the Almighty – Jehovah first appeared to Moses – why did he appear to him in a burning bush?

> *'And Moses kept the flock of Jethro his father in law, the PRIEST of Midian: and he led the flock to the backside of the desert, AND CAME TO THE MOUNTAIN OF GOD, even to HOREB.*

And the angel of the Lord appeared unto him in a flame of fire out of the midst of the bush: and he looked, and behold, the bush burned with fire, and the bush was not consumed...

And God called unto him out of the midst of the bush .... and said, I am the God of thy father, the God of Abraham, the God of Isaac, and the God of Jacob.'

(EXODUS 3: 1-6)

In this event there was no visible manifestation of God <u>as 'a personage'</u> – God did not appear to Moses in the shape of a man – but as a fire! And <u>the 'fire' spoke to Moses</u> – Why? Because that is how the Ancients looked upon God. The mountain upon which this took place was THE MOUNTAIN OF GOD – at Sinai – it was not any old mountain – it was an Ancient 'GORSEDD' or 'Sacred Place of Assembly' – forbidden except on the occasions of assembly for worship – but it seems that some of the flock which Moses was tending had strayed up the mountain – as goats will – leading Moses to the 'Sacred Place' on the Summit. **'And Moses hid his face; for he was afraid to look upon God'.** To Moses – the 'fire' in the bush was God.

Some years later, on the Route of the Exodus, Moses assembled the Twelve Tribes around this same 'Gorsedd' or 'Sacred Place of Assembly'.

'That was altogether on smoke, because the Lord descended upon it in fire: and the smoke thereof ascended as the smoke of a FURNACE, and the whole mount quaked greatly.

And when the 'voice' of the trumpet sounded long, and waxed louder and louder, Moses spake, AND GOD ANSWERED HIM '<u>BY A VOICE</u>'

(EXODUS 19: 17-19)

And there at the 'fire mount' according to the primitive custom of the Scythian Race, the Lord revealed unto them his Laws.

Up to this time, from the calling of Moses in the 'burning bush' to the Assembly of the Twelve Tribes at Sinai, Jehovah had only spoken 'by voice', both to Moses and Aaron and the people. You can read all the Chapters from Exodus 3 to Exodus 23, and you will find that God spoke to them 'by voice' only. It is not until we read Exodus Chapter 24 do we find the Lord revealing himself 'AS A PERSON', even then he appeared as a manifestation of 'heavenly fire'.

> *'Then went up Moses, and Aaron, Nabad, and Abihu, and seventy of the elders of Israel:*
>
> *And they say, saw the God of Israel: and there was under his <u>feet</u> as it were a paved work of <u>sapphire stone</u>, and as it were the '<u>body of heaven</u>' in his clearness.*
>
> *And upon the Nobles of the Children of Israel he laid not his <u>hand</u>: also they saw God and did eat and drink.*

(EXODUS 24: 9-11)

Just prior to this 'personal appearance', the people of Israel had made a Solemn Covenant 'sealed with blood' to be obedient to God's Laws revealed in the previous Chapters, i.e. 20 to 23. By the 'Blood of the Covenant' they had said:- **'All that the Lord hath said we will do, and be obedient'.**

This was, metaphorically speaking, a 'marriage' covenant – Jehovah the husband promising to Love, Honour, Cherish and Keep 'her', His 'wife' Israel, and she in turn promising 'to obey' his laws. This relationship of that as man and wife is the theme of the whole relationship.

> *'For thy Maker is thine 'HUSBAND', the 'Lord of Hosts' is his name; and thy Redeemer the Holy One of Israel;*
>
> *The God of the Whole Earth shall he be called;*
>
> *For the Lord hath called thee as a woman forsaken and grieved in spirit, and a 'WIFE' of youth, when thou wast refused, saith thy God.*

For a small moment have I forsaken thee, but with great mercies will I gather thee;

In a little wrath, I hid my face from thee for a moment; but with everlasting kindness will I have mercy on thee, saith the Lord thy Redeemer;

For this is as the waters of Noah unto me; for as I have sworn that the waters of Noah should no more go over the earth; so have I sworn that I would not be wrath with thee nor rebuke thee;

For the mountains shall depart, and the hills be removed; but my kindness shall not depart from thee;

Neither shall the covenant of my peace be removed, saith the Lord that hath mercy on thee ....

No weapon that is formed against thee shall prosper; and every tongue that shall rise against thee in judgement thou shalt condemn;

This is the heritage of the servants of the Lord, and their righteousness is of me, saith the Lord.'

(ISAIAH 54: 5-17)

So here upon the 'fire mount' of Sinai, the Lord revealed 'himself' to her in the personage of his spirit as the 'body of heaven' in his clearness (meaning he appeared as the brightness of the Sun – 'the Fire of Heaven') – standing as it were upon a paved work of Sapphire stone. Sapphire is crystal blue in colour – just as 'blue heat' would appear when a fire is at great temperature!

And in the Scripture above – through the Prophet Isaiah almost eight hundred and fifty years later, the Lord re-affirms his covenant to his 'wife' even in her sins!

According to Dr Roger O'Connor:-

'The Ancient Scythian word BRI-TETHGNE, pronounced BRI-TINNI, means 'the fire hill'.

To illustrate the true meaning of this word, it will be necessary to state the Ancient Institution of the Scythian Race, which gave rise to it.

In every Commune of the Scythian Lands, there was a Small Mount, either natural or artificial, nigh unto which was a permanent 'booth' (name for dwelling), the only one in the district, wherein dwelt the individual whose office it was to guard a portion of Sacred Elementary Fire, to prevent its being extinguished, and also to kindle therefrom an artificial fire on the summit of the Adjoining Mount, the signal for assembling the people of the Commune for the purpose of transacting their affairs, and which continued to burn whilst the congregation abided there about.

This hill was called 'BRI', THEGNE which due to changes in pronunciation was pronounced 'BRI-TINNI' or 'BRI-TAINI'!

In respect, therefore Mount Sinai was a BRI-TINNI! 'BRIT' or 'BRITH' in Ancient Hebrew means Covenant, and 'TINNI' means Mount, so the whole means, 'Hill of the Covenant'.

Was not also the contest between Elijah and the Prophets of Baal a contest of which 'Fire God' was the true God!

The contest took place on the 'Bri-tinni' of Mount Carmel. After the Prophets of Baal had failed to bring down the 'Sacred Fire' upon the altar, Elijah took Twelve Stones, according to the number of the Tribes, and with the Stones he built an Altar, made a trench around it, and using four barrels of water soaked the whole three times. And at the time of the offering of the evening sacrifice Elijah called the 'Sacred Fire' down, then the 'Fire of the Lord' fell, and consumed the Burnt Sacrifice, and the Wood, and the Stones, and licked up the Water that was in the Trench. And when all the people saw it, they fell on their faces and said, The Lord he is God, the Lord he is God! (1 Kings Chapter 18).

And again, in the 'PILLAR OF FIRE' which preceded the camp of Israel in the Wilderness, the personification of God was manifest.

These, and over three hundred other Scriptural References of this theme could be demonstrated.

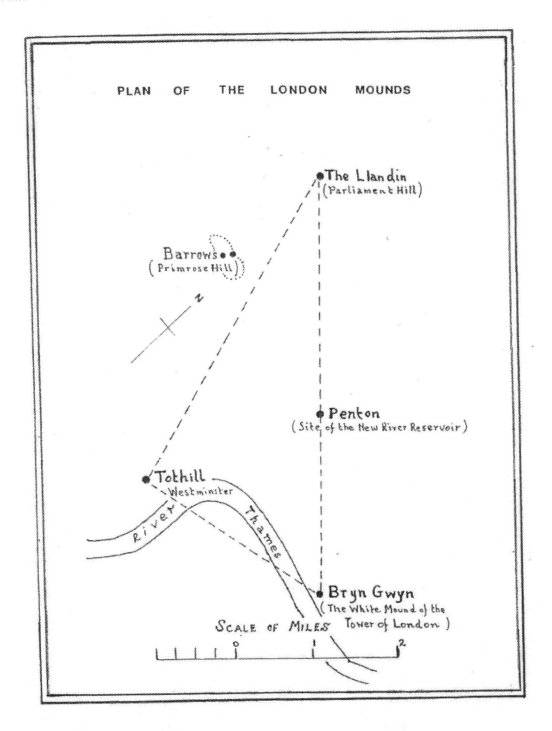

Fig. 6: Plan of the London Gorsedd Mounds

CHAPTER FOUR

The Spanish Connection
Part One
Migration of the Tribe of Judah and Dan

Who are the Hebrews?

When we refer to the chart in this Chapter, we will see that Jacob-Israel had twelve sons, and that one, and one only of them bears the name Judah.

If all of the descendants of Judah had formed themselves into one tribe (which they did not, and will be shown later) then the Judahites would have consisted of 1/12th part of the Nation of Israel, and never at any time all of it, as some people appear to contend.

Some of the people who are known as Jews are descended from Judah. But the Jews do not represent all of the House of Judah; the name 'Jew' comes from the Hebrew 'Yehudim' which means 'Remnant of Judah'; and that is exactly what the Jews (that portion who are really descended from Judah) are – a remnant of Judah. A remnant of one of the Twelve Tribes of Israel.

All Jews are not Israelites. Millions merely adopted the Jewish Religion which did not in any sense of the word change their Racial Origin. In ESTHER 8: 17 we are told, **'Many of the people of the land became Jews';** Jews did not make them Israelites. It is estimated that there are twenty million Jews in the world today. It is doubtful if as many as 20% of them are of Judah descent. Many are of heathen origin drawn into that faith long ago as proselytes (Matt 23: 15).

Many Edomites (descendants of Esau) adopted the Jewish Religion about one hundred and twenty five years before Christ, when their Kingdom was destroyed by the Nation of the Jews (See 1 Kings 11; 2 Kings 8: 20; 2 Chronicles 21: 8-10).

The Encyclopaedia Britannica states that a whole Nation of people who lived around the Black and Caspian Seas, in what we call Russia today, who were known as the Khazars of Chazara adopted the Jewish Religion about the 8th Century AD. These people were of Mongolian stock. Their change of religion did not make them Israelites. Most of the Russian Jews are descended from these Khazars. They are known among Jewry as ASKENAZIM JEWS. They are not racially descended from Judah nor from any of the Tribes of Israel. A genuine Jew is one who is descended from Judah. But many other people are also descended from Judah who are not Jews, as we shall see as we proceed.

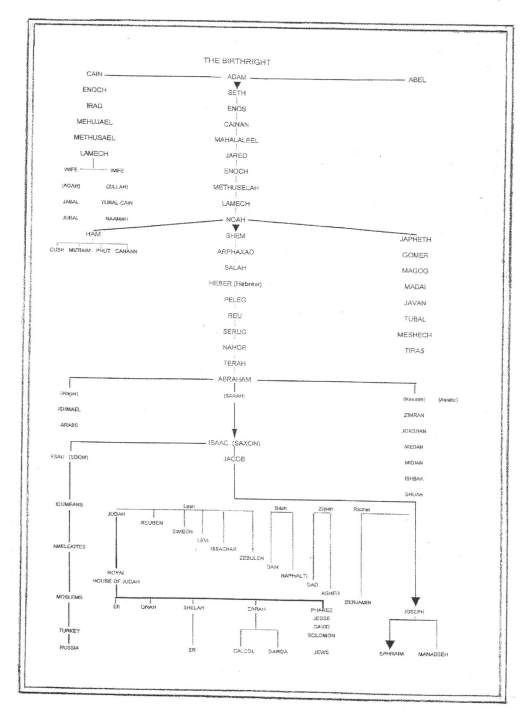

Fig. 7: Chart: The Birthright Nations – (Chart 1)

As we have stated before, we must not make the mistake of thinking that all Hebrews are 'Jews', or that all Israelites are 'Jews'. The Racial Descent was as follows:-

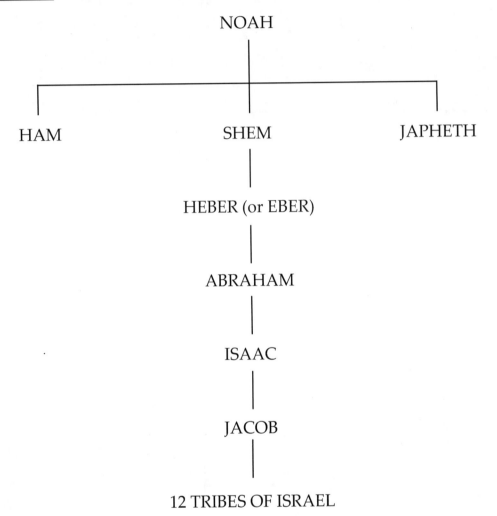

```
                        NOAH
                          |
      ┌───────────────────┼───────────────────┐
      |                   |                   |
     HAM                 SHEM              JAPHETH
                          |
                   HEBER (or EBER)
                          |
                      ABRAHAM
                          |
                        ISAAC
                          |
                        JACOB
                          |
                 12 TRIBES OF ISRAEL
```

They were all <u>Shemites</u> or Semites being descended from SHEM the son of NOAH. It can thus be easily seen how grossly mis-applied are the terms Semite-Semitic and Anti-Semitic. <u>ALL</u> descendants of Shem are Semitic not merely a tiny remnant of the one tribe of Judah which we call Jews.

<u>They were all Hebrews</u> being descended from HEBER who was the first HEBER-EW (Genesis 11: 15). In fact, Abraham was called – an Hebrew (Genesis 14: 13) and this was long before the birth of Judah or the 'Jewish' people! In fact all literal descendants of HEBER (or EBER) can rightly be called Semitic and Hebrew, and more particularly those descended from Judah can be called Hebrews. This title is not limited to that one tribe of people. All the true descendants of EPHRAIM-MANASSEH-DAN-NAPHTALI-ZEBULON-SIMEON-GAD-ASHER-REUBEN-ISSACHAR-SIMEON-LEVI-BENJAMIN are also HEBREWS (but not JEWS) wherever they are to be found in the world today.

So we could rightly state that the Celtic Anglo Saxon English speaking people today are Hebrews who live in the Hebrew (Heberides) Islands. And this applies to their descendants in the Commonwealth and America. They are also Semitic and Israelitish. This may come as a shock to most people; nevertheless, it is true.

Israel's Blindness

Paul said:

> *'Blindness in part is happened to Israel, until the fullness of the gentiles be come in.'*

> (Romans 11: 25)

Britain and America have been in a blinded condition for over two thousand five hundred years. Blinded to their identity, blinded to their great heritage, blinded as to their privileges, responsibilities, and mission. This blinded condition is now being removed and thousands upon thousands of our people now know who they are, and from whence they descended, and whom they ought to serve. But, nationally, we are still blinded in part, we still lack discernment and appreciation and, like Esau, do not realise the great value of our birthright and are therefore despising it.

It is quite impossible to read intelligently and understand the Bible until the difference is known between the various classes of Israelites. We must get our definitions straight – we must not ascribe statements made concerning the 'Jews' to any other people than the Jews themselves. To break this rule results in chaos, which utterly blinds the reader to any intelligent understanding of the Bible Story and of God's Great Plan and Purpose for all the Families of the Earth. Because this rule has been broken, chaotic conditions now exist in religious circles where over three hundred different denominations are teaching their own man-made ideas instead of the plain statements of Scripture.

There are five classes of Israelites mentioned in the Bible:-

1. The Ten Tribed Nation of Israel; The Northern Kingdom;

    The House of Israel.

2. The Two Tribed Nation of Judah; The Southern Kingdom;

    The House of Judah.

3. The House of David, which was taken out of the Tribe of

    Judah and set up as a separate entity to reign over the

    Twelve Tribes forever.

4. The Jews who are Israelites racially.

5. 'Spiritual Israel'; that is, all people regardless of race,

    colour, sex, or social position who have accepted Jesus

    Christ as their Saviour and entered the True Covenant

    through the Waters of Baptism. All such are adopted into

    The House of Israel.

And, as Paul puts it in Galatians 3:29, **'If ye be Christ's, then are ye Abraham's seed, and heirs according to the promise'.**

Migrations of the Tribe of Judah

Judah the man, had five sons – three of them by the daughter of SHUAH the Canaanite; namely ER, ONAN, SHELAH (Genesis 38: 2-5). The rest of the Chapter records the death of ER and ONAN SHELAH, who later became the Father of a son whom he named ER.

Judah's other two sons, born of TAMAR, his daughter-in-law, were twins named ZARAH and PHAREZ.

The story of the birth of these twin sons found in GENESIS 38 should be carefully read because therein lies the record of the disruption within the Family of Judah.

The midwife, waiting for the birth and knowing that twins were to be born, was prepared to mark the first born, because through him it was naturally expected that the Birthright, Tribal and Regal Blessings would pass.

> *'And it came to pass when she travailed; that the one put out his hand; and the midwife took and bound upon his hand a scarlet thread, saying, "This came out first". And it came to pass, as he drew back his hand, that, behold, his brother came out; and she said, "How hast thou broken forth? <u>This breach</u> be upon thee": Therefore his name was called Pharez. And afterwards came out his brother, that had the scarlet thread upon his hand, and his name was called Zarah.'*

(GENESIS 38: 27-30)

From ZARAH came CALCOL (or CHALCOL) and DARDA (or DARA) 1 Chron 2: 6, 1 Kings 4: 31.

From PHAREZ came the line of JESSE, DAVID, SOLOMON (Matthew 1: 3-16).

The JUDAH Section of the ISRAELITE Chart therefore, now looks like this:-

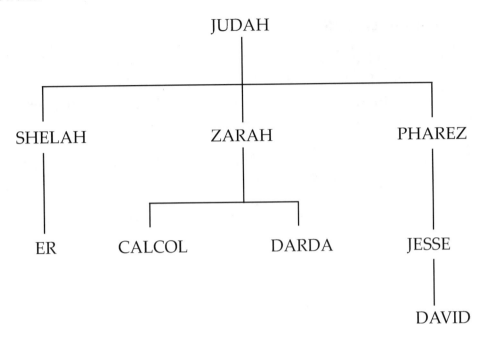

Of the three sons now under consideration, SHELAH was the firstborn, but was rejected from inheriting the Birthright Blessings due, in part, to his Mother being a Canaanite, which would have contaminated the Blood Line of the Messiah. Israelites had been forbidden to inter-marry with Canaanites – see Genesis 24: 3, 37; Deut 7: 1-6; Deut 20: 16-18. This, to his discredit the man JUDAH had done.

In GENESIS 49: 10 we are informed that, **'the Sceptre shall not depart from Judah until Shiloh come'.**

The 'Sceptre' represented the Monarchy or Royal Line. It was from the Line of Judah that the Kings of Israel should descend and eventually give birth to the Messiah (Shiloh) Jesus Christ.

So we can well understand the rivalry between SHELAH, ZARAH and PHAREZ.

SHELAH claimed the honour through being the actual firstborn son. ZARAH claimed the honour through being the son of the 'Scarlet Thread'. PHAREZ claimed the honour by being the firstborn son of TAMAR.

Shelah also bore deep resentment toward Judah, his Father, because he had not kept his word regarding the giving of TAMAR, a pure Hebrew girl, to him for his wife, which had given TAMAR the excuse to 'play the harlot' to JUDAH and which resulted in the birth of ZARAH and PHAREZ.

What a dilemma! However, it seems that the matter was settled in favour of PHAREZ, which decision, of course, was not received with the approval or acceptance of the descendants of SHELAH or ZARAH.

And so it was, that the 'BREACH' occurred as predicted by the midwife, but God has his own way of working things out – as we shall see.

Most of the descendants of SHELAH and ER left Egypt about <u>1700 BC</u>, before the Bondage Period and retraced their path across Sinai to the Lands of the Canaanites and Phoenicians, inter-marrying with them and strengthening the strain of Canaanite blood in their veins handed down from SHUA's daughter. In these Lands they learned the habits, language and superstitions of the Canaanites and Phoenicians. They also became deft in the art of seamanship for which the Phoenicians were renowned. They travelled to many lands on trading missions, some of them settling in these lands and integrating in their new homes never to return. Some settled in AFRICA, others in SPAIN and IRELAND.

Much confusion exists regarding the Phoenicians. Although Modern Historians refer to them as 'Canaanites' they were of the same Semitic Stock as Abraham, generally they were tall men with red hair and blue eyes. They were not 'Jews' as we know the word today, but a 'Celtic' people, in fact the word 'Phoenician' is not the name they called themselves, but rather a nickname which means 'red-headed men'. It is believed they were the inventors of the alphabet sometime around 1500 BC. However, the Phoenicians employed Canaanite labourers in their ships and consequently there was an infusion of blood and customs.

About the same time that SHELAH's descendants arrived in Southern Ireland, or a little before, we find that CALCOL of the ZARAH-JUDAH line had founded a colony in ULSTER.

Descendants of Calcol in Spain and Ireland

The World's Oldest Highway is the Ocean, and Historic Records tell of the Westward Migration of the descendants of CALCOL along the shores of the Mediterranean Sea, establishing IBERNIAN – EBERIAN (HEBREW) Trading Settlements, one being 'ZARAH – GASSA' meaning 'The Stronghold of Zarah' now called 'ZARAGOZA' in the EBRO Valley in Spain. Camden's 'HISTORIA BRITANNICA' states that Calcol sailed from Spain and continued onwards as far as Ireland, where they established a settlement which they named ULLADH (ULSTER) about 1600 BC. Several Ancient Records, such as 'THE ANNALS OF IRELAND' by the Four Masters (2 Volumes), the Irish 'LEABHAR GADHALA', or 'Book of Conquests', and including 'THE CHRONICLES OF ERI', now under consideration, point to these 'IBERII' (IBERIANS) as being some of the earliest inhabitants of Spain and Ireland.

Including also in these records is the account of another fierce tribe named the TUATHA DE DANAAN (Tribe of Dan) who invaded Ireland about 1200 BC.

Thus the Iber-nians or Iberi who settled in Spain and Ireland were undoubtedly Hebrews, descended from Abraham through Judah's sons Zarah/Calcol, and while from the stock of Judah are certainly not 'Jews'.

A Modern Apostle Testifies

Elder Anthony W Ivins, an Apostle and 1st Counsellor to Heber J Grant has commented:-

> 'Under King Solomon, Israel realized her Golden Age. Tribute was collected from all surrounding Nations. ADONIRAM (ADORAM) was his Collector of Taxes. He also served in this capacity under Solomon's son REHOBOAM after the latter succeeded to the throne.

At ZARAGOZA, in Spain, there is a tombstone with the following inscription:-

> **'This is the tomb of Adoniram, the servant of King Solomon, who came to collect tribute and died here.'**

Now turn to your Bible, 1 Kings 4: 6 and 12: 18. It shows that this man Adoniram (or Adoram) was sent into Spain to collect tribute, and all Israel rose up and stoned him to death. 'Therefore Rehoboam made speed to get him up to his chariot to flee to Jerusalem'.

Rehoboam commenced his rule about 975 BC. This makes plain the fact that almost one thousand years before Christ, Israel had extended its Empire as far as Spain.

Elder Ivins then continues with a review of Historical Documents that indicate that the Tribe of DAN had also extended its influence and trade to the – then known, British Isles and Scandinavian Countries of Europe, 1,000 BC!

Anthony W Ivins, 'The Lost Tribes' (A personal letter on file at BYU #Mor, M238 2 IV 51) Early 1900s – fifteen pages:-

DARDA

'Many of the DARDA branch of these ZARAH-JUDAHITES left Egypt and settled themselves in Asia Minor along the DARDA-NELLS as it is still known today, and the HEBRUS RIVER in Ancient Thrace. This latter branch of Judah founded the Ancient City of Troy. Some hundreds of years later came the famous 'Siege of Troy' which was destroyed by the 'DANOI' of Greece, 1183 BC. These Danoi were of the Tribe of Dan, which had split into three sections or more, and about one-third of them had populated Greece, so it was really blood brothers of the 'TROJANS' who had ruined their City, although in all probability, unknown to either of them at the time.

Following the destruction of Troy, AENEAS the last of the Royal Blood, collected the remnants of his Nation and travelled with them into Italy. Later, his great-grandson BRUTUS, or BRIT, migrated with many of his followers to Malta and eventually to Britain.

We find success attending this immigration of the King and his people and he eventually landed with some followers on these shores at TORBAY. An Historic Stone still stands in the Ancient Town of TOTNES, Devon, commemorating his coming. It stands in FORE STREET and has been plainly marked 'BRUTUS STONE', but alas few people today know of the great History it symbolizes. Also in St. Peter's Church on Cornhill, London, is a Stone Tablet attesting to the arrival of the Trojans about 1075 BC. Traces of Trojans have also been found in Scotland. Brutus built for himself a New Capital City to which he gave the name 'CAER TROIA' or 'NEW TROY'. The Romans later called it LONDINIUM, now known as London.

The escape of AENEAS with his family and followers to Italy and subsequent story of the adventures of his great-grandson Brutus are related to us in the 'Old British Chronicles'.

These are handed down to us through Latin translations made by the British Christian Scholars: GILDAS ALBANIUS 500 AD, NENNIUS 900 AD and BISHOP GEOFFREY of MONMOUTH 1150 AD. Our information is quoted from Geoffrey's version, translated from the Latin into English by A Thompson of Oxford in 1718 AD and reproduced by J Giles into Modern English.

The brief synopsis given here demonstrates almost unquestionably that the earliest inhabitants of these Islands were descendants of HEBER, ABRAHAM, ISAAC, JACOB and were actually here long before the re-gathering and settlement of the Ten-Tribed Israel in these Islands which took place about 2000 to 1500 years later, i.e. around about 500 AD. These early settlers were therefore all here BEFORE Isaiah wrote (about 800 BC) and even 1000 years or so BEFORE the ten tribes were taken into captivity in Assyria and 1200 years or so BEFORE Lehi left Jerusalem (600 BC)!

To them Isaiah sends great predictions concerning the Mighty Nation of which they were to be forerunners. He speaks to them of the coming of their brethren in later times, of the expansion of a future world-wide Empire, and above all, of its influence for God in the World as a Great Missionary People or Servant Nation, to be God's witnesses as a Nation, and to be a Light eventually to enlighten and lead all other people into the ways of God's truth and laws.

So we find DARDA-JUDAH very much alive in Britain and while they are Hebrews of the stock of JUDAH they are certainly not 'Jews'.

Israel's Waymarks and High Heaps and The Migrations of the Tribe of Dan

Speaking to Ephraim, the Eternal says in JEREMIAH 31: 20-21:-

'Set thee up '<u>waymarks</u>', make thee '<u>high heaps</u>':

Set thine heart toward the highway, <u>even the way which thou wentest</u>'.

From this instruction we should expect some kind of 'signs' or 'waymarks' to have been left along the trail by which the Ancient Hebrews journeyed.

Dan the Serpent's Trail

In GENESIS 49: 17, JACOB foretelling what should befall each of the Tribes, says:- **'DAN SHALL BE A SERPENT BY THE WAY'**, or **'DAN SHALL BE A SERPENT'S TRAIL'**. It is a significant fact that the Tribe of Dan named every place they settled after their Father DAN. A few points in the History of the DAN-ITES will show as how they became a Serpent's Trail.

The Tribe of Dan originally occupied a strip of Coastal Country on the Mediterranean – West of Jerusalem. But this division of the land soon became too small for the tribe, as we are told in the following, JOSHUA 19: 47:-

> *'The coast of the children of Dan went out too little for them; therefore the children of Dan went up to fight against Leshem, and took it ....*
> *and called Leshem, Dan, after the name of their father'.*

Also in JUDGES 18: 11-12 it is recorded that the Danites took **KIRJATHJERIM**, and 'called the place **MAHANEH-DAN** unto this day'.

Some time later a Company of six hundred armed Danites came to LAISH, captured it, and 'they called the name of the City Dan, after the name of DAN their Father' (Verse 29).

So we notice how these Danites left their 'Serpent's Trail' by the way – set up 'Waymarks' by which may be traced to this day.

As we have already mentioned the Ancient Hebrew contained no vowels – (A,E,I,O,U). The vowel sound being supplied in the pronunciation. Thus the word DAN in its English equivalent could be spelled simply 'DN'. It may therefore be pronounced 'DAN', 'DEN', 'DIN', 'DON', 'DUN', and still could be the original Hebrew name.

It is recorded that DAN abode in ships, JUDGES 5: 17. Therefore, the DAN-ITES were principally seamen – just like the Phoenicians, in fact, much of their commercial seagoing activities were joint ventures, so it is not surprising to find their Trading Colonies to be occupied by both groups.

Just before his death Moses prophesied of DAN: **'DAN IS A LION'S WHELP: HE SHALL LEAP FROM BASHAN'** (Deut 33: 22). Along the shores of the Mediterranean they left their 'trail' in names 'DAR-DAN-ELLS', 'ME-DIN-A', 'SI-DON-IA', 'SAR-DIN-IA', etc.

We find these 'Waymarks' all over Europe and the British Isles.

In their Overland Route we find the name 'DAN' in the rivers DNIEPER, DNIESTER and DON. Then in either Ancient or Later Geography we find DAN-UBE, the DAN-INN, the DAN-ASTER, the DAN-DARI, the DAN-EZ, the U-DON, and ERI-DON.

Leading to their destination of DEN-MARK. Denmark means – 'DAN'S-MARK', meaning 'Dan's last resting place'. We also find their identity in SCAN-<u>DIN</u>-AVIANS.

<u>In Ireland</u> we find these 'Waymarks' in: - DANS-LAUGH, DAN-SOWER, DUN-DALK, DUN-DRUM, DON-EGAL BAY, DUN-EGAL CITY, DUN-GLOW, LON-DON-DERRY. There is also DIN-GLE, DUN-GARVEN, and DUN'S-MORE (which means 'MORE DAN'S'). Moreover the name DUN in ERSE, the Ancient Irish Language, means the same as DAN in the Hebrew. Judge, DAN-I-EL which means the Judge of God.

In Scotland, as in Ireland, we find these Waymarks in the names of DUN-DEE, DUN-RAVEN, E-DIN-BURGH. In England:- DON-CASTER, LON-DON, in fact there are literally hundreds.

<u>ELDUD</u>, an eminent Jewish writer said:-

> 'In Jeroboam's day (975 BC) Dan refused to shed his brother's blood, and rather than go to war with the people of Judah, he left the Country and went in a body to Greece, then to Javin (Spain) – (and sometimes referred to as the British Isles), and then to Denmark.'

<u>KEATING'S History of Ireland</u> says:-

> 'The Danaans were a people of great learning and wealth; they left Greece after a battle with the Assyrians and went to Ireland, and also to Danmark, and called it 'DAN-MARES', Dan's country.'

In the 'ANNALS OF IRELAND' we find:-

> 'The Danaans were a highly civilized people, well skilled in architecture and other arts from their long residence in Greece. Their first appearance in Ireland was 1200 BC.'

It is also a well authenticated fact of history that the Milesians, or 'Scots', inhabited the North of Ireland, as well as the Tribe of Dan, and that they were the same race of people. The word SCOT in Hebrew meaning 'wanderers' or 'dwellers in booths', or tents, of which the Israelites were well noted (LEV 23: 42). And to the Gaal Sciot of Iber it meant 'Archers'.

The 'CLANS' of Scotland gives note of a tribal beginning, as does the plaid of the multi-coloured kilt identify this Nation with the coat of many colours of Joseph the son of Jacob.

The 'archers' of the 'wanderers' who 'dwell in tents' who wear the multi-coloured kilt!

Therefore between 1600 BC to 1200 BC Ireland was occupied by three Clans.

1. The ZARAH/CALCOL BRANCH OF JUDAH

2. The Tuatha de Danaan – descendants of DAN

3. The SHELAH/JUDAH Canaanite Phoenicians and Semitic

   Phoenicians.

They named their New Island Home 'IERNE' or 'HIBERNIA', the latter term coming from 'HEBER' or 'EBER' – the Father of the HEBER-EWS. The Islands to the North were named 'HEBERIDIES' and are called the 'HEBRIDES' today, 'The Islands of the Hebrews'. Later the name was changed to ERI or ERI-LAND – from this we have the modern name IRELAND today, or EIRE, pronounced 'ERIE'. The Ancient Irish Language was 'ERSE' – a combination of Hebrew and Phoenician.

The name SHELAH or 'SHELAGH' (Son of JUDAH) and its derivatives are popular in both Ireland and Scotland. One famous Irish Ballad mentions the SHELALAH, a kind of Irish walking stick.

In 1 CHRONICLES 4: 21-23 we find the descendants of SHELAH and ER, his son, described as being skilled workers in fine linen, pottery, plants and hedges. This would almost describe the inhabitants of Modern Ireland. Almost everyone has heard of fine Irish Linen and Belleek China, and the Irishman loves his garden!

The Canaanite infusion of blood may also account for SINN-FEIN (a title taken from <u>FENIAN</u> – PHOENICIAN) Irish animosity towards the British. This animosity is only to be found in the populace of Southern Ireland or Republican element towards those who dwell in Ulster and Britain, which, on the surface, seems inexplicable. However, we are told in the Scriptures that the Canaanites were to be 'pricks in the eyes, and thorns in the flesh of Semitic Ephraim/Israel' – NUMBERS 33: 55; JOSHUA 23: 12-13.

<u>Blood runs deep</u> – and although the event of the birth of JUDAH'S sons SHELAH, ZARAH and PHAREZ happened many years ago, deep down the resentment – the 'BREACH' between various factions of that family are still there. The descendants of SHELAH resenting the loss of the Birthright. It may sound unbelievable to think that this could be the cause of the troubles in Ireland today, but I believe this is the '<u>root</u>' cause, no matter how fantastic it may sound.

Also we find that the Irish had a peculiar habit of naming places by the name of their God, BAAL.

Now BAAL in these terms means the Babylonian God idol, not the name '<u>BAAL</u>' given to the Sun by the Gaal-Sciot-Iber in the 'Chronicles of Eri'.

We find in Ireland literally dozens of names including the name BAAL – BALLY-MENA, BALLY-KELLY, BALLY-MURPHY, BELFAST (BEL being a derivative of BAAL) is also predominant in many words. Even DUBLIN'S Ancient Name, BAILE-ATHA-CLAITH means 'place of BAAL'!

Also the small Islands of the West Coast of Ireland are named AR-AN (ER-AN). The ERRIGAL ('ERI-GAL') mountains in the North West. Logh ERNE ('LAKE ER-NE). The districts of AR-MAGH ('ER-MAGH'), AR-AN-MORE ('ER-AN-MORE') and F-ER-MANAGH ('ER-MANAGH'), the place of the Fergneat, or aborigines. Also the Irish Ballad 'DANNY' BOY still sung to this day!

Eventually, even many years later, the descendants of ZARAH/CALCOL and those of the Tribe of DAN integrated into one people sharing the Northern part of Ireland.

They became known as 'CALCOL-DAN-IANS', which was shortened to 'CALDANIANS', and eventually 'CAL-E-DON-IANS', or 'CALEDONIANS', which simply means the people of CALCOL and DAN, and in later history, the word 'SCOT' being added. Then they migrated to what we know as SCOT-LAND today, they called it 'CALEDONIA'! and became known as the CALEDONIAN SCOTS, or ('GAEL-E-DON-IA' – 'The GAEL AND DAN-IANS').

It is well known to those who have seen and studied the people of Ireland that there are two distinct Races there, those who are of the old MILESIAN Race, and many of SCAN-DIN-AVIAN and I-SAXON extraction who are all kindred peoples who mostly settled in the North and North West. There is another class of Irish people, especially in the South and South West, who are quite distinct, judging from their physique, character, and habits, and customs, and who have been long bound down in ignorance and superstition that they have not been able to make such progress as the peoples of the North. Their physique and character favour the belief that they are of the Phoenician/Canaanite Ancestry.

'Feine' was the name of the people under Sidonian Rule, and EIS-FEINE was the name given to the part of Spain under the same dominion. These names Feine and Eis-Feine. <u>Fenian</u>, the old title of the people of Southern Ireland, is a derivative of this Canaanite/Phoenician Title, and by which the people of Southern Ireland respond today, and to the present title of SINN-FEIN, which has been applied to the I.R.A, a more extreme element who, with those who support them have fulfilled the prophecy that they would be as 'pricks in the eyes', and 'thorns in the sides', of the Saxon People, who without doubt are the race or descendants of I-SAAC, JACOB and ISRAEL, more especially Ephraim and Manasseh.

We shall examine these points again in a further Chapter.

SEE MAP:- 'HEBREW MIGRATIONS AND ISRAEL'S WANDERINGS'

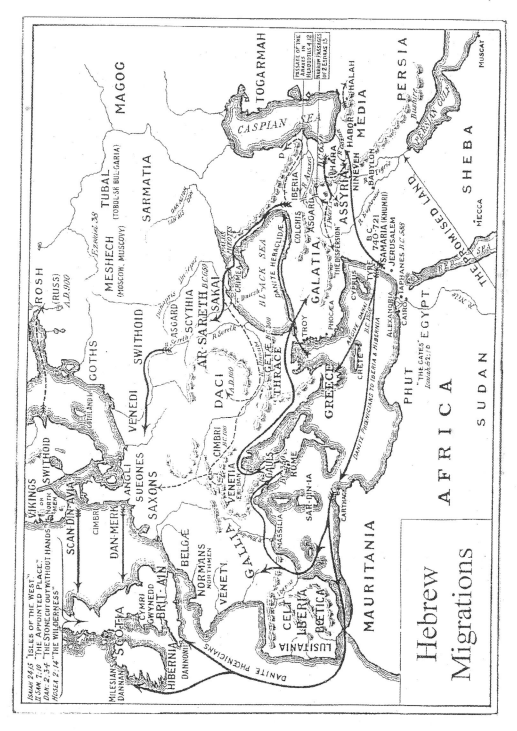

Fig. 8: Showing Phoenician-Hebrew Migrations and Trade Routes

Israel's High Heaps

The shores of the Mediterranean and Atlantic seaboard are dotted with megalithic stone shrines. As the people who set them up moved further on, their ideas evidently expanded and so we have the great stone circles of Stonehenge and Avebury in England, and Callernish in the Hebrides. The period for the erection of these Circles is given as 1800 BC, under the leadership of Hu-Gadarn, known as Hu the Mighty.

A traditional custom that indelibly bound the Kelts, Celts and Gaels (the meaning of the word in each case is stranger) indicating they were strangers or wanderers to the land which they rested on their trek to the Isles. Today their passage across the World can be clearly traced by the relics of the altars they raised in Stone, enduring memorials to their great pilgrimage.

This tradition lingers today, and, as then, only among the Keltic-Saxon people. In our times the custom of erecting these memorials to some great historic event is chiefly practiced by the Scots and Canadians.

They comprise Pyramids of Stone piled to a peak and are known as 'CAIRNS'. This is the Keltic name for the word used in the Bible as 'Heaps', 'Stones of Witness', and were normally erected to a height of four to six feet.

The first Stone Altar in the Biblical Record was erected by Jacob after his significant dream of the Ascending Ladder between heaven and earth, known as Jacob's Ladder. He built it as a witness to this contact and covenant with God on that occasion GENESIS 28 and GENESIS 31: 45-46.

So also does Scripture mention Stone Circles, for we find in the Fourth Chapter of Joshua that the Lord commanded Joshua to erect a Circle of Twelve Stones at Gilgal, which means 'Circle' (JOSHUA 4:19-21).

Ever after the erection of such Altars (Cairns) or Stone Circles became a Religious Custom of the wandering Hebrew and Keltoi as they passed through strange lands, a declaration and a witness to their belief and faith in the covenant with the one and only Eternal God.

In contrast to the Pyramid Type Stone Heaps or 'Cairns' were the 'High Mounds', formed from natural or artificial grass covered mounds up to five hundred feet in height. Upon the summit were erected twelve standing stones with a larger one in the centre, the MAENLLOG or LLOGAN Stone, which was symbolic of the Tabernacle of the Rock of Christ.

The Cymric word 'GORSEDD' means 'High Seats' which term was applied to the Seat of the Monarchs, or 'Place of Assembly', where the King or Chieftain, the Clergy, and the Freemen assembled and enacted the Law and Justice. Those early Keltic 'Gorsedds' were the first Parliaments of a free people. Keltic tradition has said that it was within the 'Circles of Avebury' that the Gorsedds were instituted, a National Institution not known outside of Britain. In the National Gorsedds and Eisteddfods of Wales the traditions of the Druidic Assemblies on the Wiltshire downs survive to this day.

The Cymric words 'TON – 'TOT' – 'TOTE' and 'TOR' signify a Sacred Mount. The word 'Circle' in the Ancient British Tongue was 'COR' and in those 'CORS' they gathered. The word has come down to us in our 'COURT', and in another sense in the word 'CHOIR'.

The approach to the 'COR' or summit of the High Place was reached by 'Serpent-like Avenues' in the form of a Footpath, or Avenue of Stones. The Avenues at Avebury are several miles long.

The words 'TON' – 'TOT' and 'TOR' survive unto this day. The Tower of London with which is connected so much of the romance of the British History, was erected on the site of the Ancient Celtic White Mount, the 'BRYN GWYN' in the Welsh Language (BRYN – 'hill', GWYN – 'white') – White Hill.

Some miles North of the Tower was the Llandin from the Welsh Llan, 'Sacred' and 'Din', 'Eminence', meaning a High Place of Worship. Llandin is also the original derivation of London.

Two miles West of the Tower, near where Westminster Abbey now stands, was another 'High Place' with a circle and a Druidic College, named TOTHILL.

The hill was levelled after the reign of Elizabeth I, but the name still survives in 'TOTHILL STREET', and 'TOTHILL FIELDS'.

These London Mounds referred to were from one hundred to three hundred feet in height and must have been with their stone circles, striking monuments in pre-historic London, towering like great Cathedrals above the flat landscape of the Thames Marshes. On the high ground where St. Pauls now stands, might have been silhouetted against the sky the mighty unhewn Monoliths of the Druidic Circle – however no trace of the Circle remains today.

Other Mounds or Gorsedds are to be found all over Britain. At Avebury, (Silbury Hill) (the word Avebury is derived from 'ABRI' being the Ancient form of the word Hebrews). Then twenty miles South of Avebury is Stonehenge. Its original Celtic name is COR-GAWR, or 'The Great Circle of the Ambresbiri' (The Holy Anointed Ones). And another at Glastonbury in Somerset, named 'The Glastonbury <u>Tor</u>', which is five hundred feet in height and is associated with 'Joseph of Arimathea'. And still further at Win<u>ton</u> (Winchester), and at Windsor, London, known as 'The Round Table Mound', upon which King Arthur (871 AD) re-organized the 'Old Druidic Order' on 'Christian Principles'. Later on Edward III (1328 AD) built his 'Round Tower' on 'Round Table Mound' and for many centuries 'The Assemblies of the Orders of St. George and the Garter', Britain's 'Highest Orders' have been held there.

The 'Windsor Gorsedd', 'The Win-de-sieur', 'The White, or Holy Mount of the Sieur', or 'Lord' (according to the Welsh derivation of the name), is the only Gorsedd which has unbroken historical continuity, and has literally fulfilled its Keltic Title as the 'Great Seal of the Throne of the Monarch', from the Sixth Century to the present day.

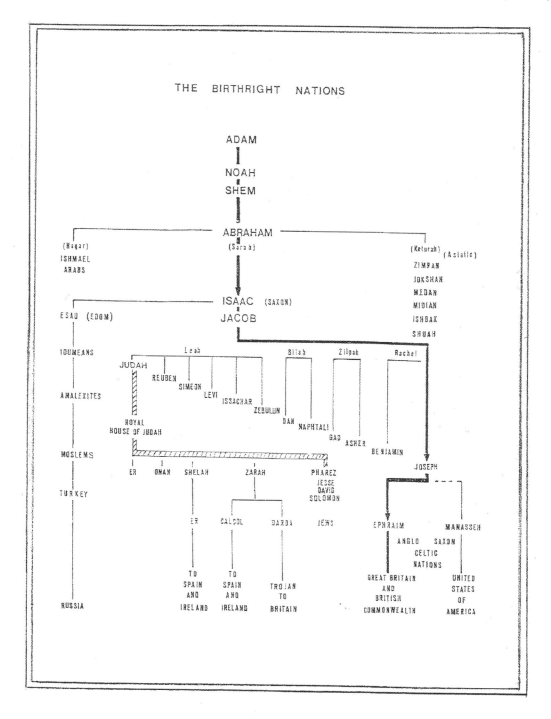

Fig. 9: Chart: The Birthright Nations – (Chart 2)

CHAPTER FIVE

The Spanish Connection
Part Two
Migrations of the Gaal-Sciot of Iber
2400 BC – 1490 BC

It must be pointed out that in the migrations of the Semite Scythians the migrations of the Gaal-Sciot of Iber was only one of many, but without doubt the most important.

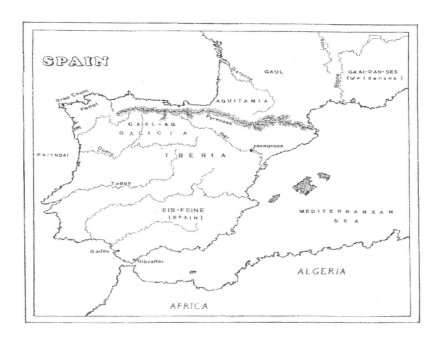

Fig. 10: Map of Spain 1500 B.C

Eolus the originator of the 'Chronicles of the Gaal-Sciot of Iber' gives his Genealogy as follows:-

Chiefs of the Gaal-Sciot of Iber – Noah to Eolus

			B.C From – To
Years	Flood in the days of NOAH	about	2563 –
	Ardfear or Noah. Death of Noah	about	– 2213
	Macaar or Iatfoth		
	Og		
	Dorca		
263	Glas	First Chief of Iber	1950 –
	File		
	Daire		1492 –
<u>458</u>	Cealgac		
	Calma		– 1475
	Ronard		
	Duil		
	Nine Heads of People		
	Enar		
107	Eolus		1368 – 1335

<u>Total 828</u>

To follow the narrative it will be necessary for the reader to make frequent reference to the Genealogies shown in the Chapter Headings – and also to the Maps and Demonstration Notes.

CHAPTER II

From the Death of ARDFEAR to the commencement of the reign of GLAS in IB-BER, a space of 263 rings.

CHAPTER III

From the commencement of GLAS, first Chief of IBER, of the race of ARD-FEAR, in 1950, to CEALGAC the son of DAIRE – a space of four hundred two score and eighteen rings.

CHAPTER IV

From the election of CEALGAC, 1492 before Christ, till the arrival of a Colony of Gaal of Sciot of IB-ER in Gael-ag, and the death of CALMA, a space of seventeen rings.

CHAPTER V

From the Death of CALMA, 1475, to the election of EOLUS, a space of 107 rings.

The above Chapter Headings are taken from the 'Chronicles', the total amount of years from the death of Ardfear (NOAH) to the election of Eolus being 828 years. If one deducts 1368 BC (the election of Eolus) from 2213 BC (death of Ardfear) the total is 845 years. The apparent discrepancy being the seventeen years which elapsed before CALMA was elected Chief of the Iber in Gael-ag of Spain.

I have included this genealogy and other facts for the reader to follow the narrative. The 'Chronicles' record only those dates shown.

The 'Chronicles' were commenced by Eolus who ruled over the Gaal-Sciot-Iber in Galacia from 1368 BC to 1335 BC.

Eolus acquired his knowledge of writing in SIDON and he selected a group of men to start the 'Chronicles' which commenced with his own reign in Galacia (Spain), and carried through to the time of Christ. These are the TRUE FACTS of the reign of each King, from his own day to the Christian Era.

The first Volume of the 'Chronicles' is headed 'THE WRITINGS OF EOLUS'.

'The Writings of Eolus' – in Volume One contain the account of his Forefathers from the time of the Flood to his day, this History is taken from Legends and other Sources acquired by Eolus. Even so, this must be a credible History due to his great integrity and wisdom. No-one who reads the 'Chronicles' can fail to be impressed by the sincerity of Eolus.

'The Chronicles of Gael-ag' – commence with Chapter Six of Volume One. This History records the affairs of the Gaal-Sciot-Iber in Gael-ag (Galacia) in Spain.

These are <u>TRUE FACTS</u> being commenced by Eolus in 1368 BC and from the time of his death in 1335 BC the History being faithfully recorded by the Ard-Olam (High Priests) unto 1007 BC

'The Chronicles of Eri' – in Volume Two are also the <u>TRUE FACTS</u>, being a continued record of the History of the Gaal-Sciot-Iber in Eri (Ireland) 1007 BC to 7 BC. After their arrival in Ireland the Gaal-Sciot of Iber changed their name to Gaal of Eri, calling their new home 'ERI'.

This information was given in the 'Exposition' but a reminder is useful at this point.

We will now continue with the 'Writings of Eolus'. In this account Eolus tells us that the Fathers of his race dwelt originally North-East of the Tigris (see Map of Western Asia), and after thirteen hundred years passed Westward towards the Euphrates and became Rulers of that Land, Ruling with Mercy. Three hundred years later a great army from the East, near to the land of their first origin, fierce and cruel, overwhelmed them and many were slain and made captive.

Ardfear, the Chief of their Race, and many of the Heads of the People, escaped by way of the Euphrates and settled in the Land of Ard-Mionn (ARMENIA). Many others from Magh-sean-ar (MESOPOTAMIA) also made their escape, and Ardfear ruled. Eisoir is the name given to this cruel conquering people, who appear to have been the early Assyrians.

When Ardfear died, his body was placed in the boat by which he had escaped up the Euphrates and conveyed on the shoulders of his Nobles nine hundred paces from the margin of the water (probably Lake Van) where he was buried and a heap of stones (Cairn) was raised over him.

'The Chronicles' give the names and a slight History of many succeeding Rulers in Ard-Mionn, and show that many other people came into the land,

and that some spread over the Caucasus Mountains, and that others spread Westwards. One such group being that of Hu-Gadarn.

The Gaal Sciot of Iber, who remained in the land greatly increased and occupied all the land between the Caspian and Black Sea, South of the Caucasus and North of Armenia. **They named the settlement IBERIA**. (*See map of Western Asia).

These Celts were descended from Shem, they excelled all the people in the use of the bow, and became experts in working mines, forging swords and making vessels of brass. They sought gold, silver and copper to use in their unique Celtic crafts. They traded with people around them.

Some of them took leave from IBERIA, travelling West to the Phoenician Port of Sidon.

About 1490 BC, when the people assembled to elect their Chief, they inclined to CALMA, son of DAIRE, but CEALGAC, his brother surrounded the place of the election with chosen bands of men, made mad with strong drink, and stirred them against the Heads (Elders) of the people, and had himself proclaimed King. He sought to slay CALMA, for he was jealous of the love of the people towards him.

CALMA remonstrated with his brother, reminding him of their kinship, and said, that if CEALGAC would promise to rule the people in Mercy and Justice, he would depart from Iber with as many as would follow him. His words pleased CEALGAC, and after one year CALMA chose nine times nine youths, each of those choosing nine others, one of every nine to take with him a wife, making a Company of more than eleven hundred. All the youths were well armed, and many others would have followed, but CALMA prevented them.

They started in a South Westerly direction. CALMA said they would go to Aoimag (HAMATH in SYRIA) to get tidings of some of their brethren who had been captured eleven years before with CUIR – under whose eye CALMA had been reared, and sold in Sgadan (SIDON).

On the seventh evening of their journey, as they were resting by the bank of a river, lo! They saw a troop of men, with damsels, moving towards them, and, as they drew near, they saw RONARD, another of CALMA'S brothers, with exactly such a number following him.

There was dancing and great joy, and, on the morrow, when CALMA would have proceeded on his way, RONARD told him he could not abide in Ib-er without him, and begged that he and his Company might share their lot. CALMA was glad, and the whole host shouted for joy when they knew that they were not to be separated.

They struck their tents and moved on towards Sgadan, but found that their brethren had been taken away to the right side of the sea (Mediterranean). NARGAL was the Chief of AOIMAG, and was inclined to deal with deception against them, and make them his slaves. The men of Sgadan agreed to find ships and to convey CALMA and his hosts to Eis-feine (SPAIN), the land which their brethren had been taken.

They made a covenant with NARGAL that if he dealt truly with them, they would pay his servants the price named for their passage by his ships, but would make no other covenant binding themselves to NARGAL in any way. They said, **'Whithersoever we go, we will live free'.**

They tarried a little time in Sgadan, NARGAL taking delight in listening to the tales of other times from the lips of FEITAM whose words were sweet. NARGAL wished FEITAM to stay in Sgadan, 'That his words might be set down on tables to endure forever'. FEITAM would not be persuaded, but promised to return at some future time, if it pleased CALMA, and the distance did not exceed the time of one moon. The Chiefs exchanged the hand of friendship and kindred, and took their departure from Sgadan (SIDON).

Gael-ag, the Spanish Colony

They sailed by way of the Mediterranean, passed through the Strait of Gibraltar, and round by the Coast of Eis-feine (SPAIN) which they entered by the mouth of the rivers Tagus and Duor, now in Portugal. They settled North of the Duor, and called their land Gael-ag (SEE MAP). Portugal is simply a derivative of PORT OF THE GAELS!

They could get no tidings of their brethren of Iber, who had been transported there from Sgadan.

They also discovered that the natives of the land, as also settlers, were expected to pay tribute to NARGAL for the freedom of mining and use of the sea, but CALMA and RONARD, with all the hosts of Iber, were of one mind, and again declared that **'They would die or live free'**. Then the servants of NARGAL told them where some of their brethren dwelt.

Eis-feine is a derivative of Phoenicians – Fenicians – Fenians – Eis-feine meaning the land of Phoenicians, which is now shortened to SPAIN.

The people of IBER – Iber-ians – named the land 'IBERIA' after their Forefather IBER – (HEBER) the 4th Patriarch from SHEM, and by which the whole of the land of Spain is known to this day. 'SPAIN' after its Phoenician settlers, and 'IBERIA' after its Hebrew – IBER-EW settlers!

CALMA and his people journey Northwards and find some of their own race who had left Iber one hundred and forty years before and settled in what is now known as the Algarve, South of Portugal.

A Company of them had journeyed seaward round the Coast and occupied the land of BUAISCE (BISCAY). These are known as the BASQUES today. CALMA and his host journeyed with them for a short time and CALMA took for his wife a daughter of the Chief of the Basques.

Afterwards the people of the Gaal Sciot of Iber spread toward the North East, settling both South and North of the Pyrenees. In the North they named the land EOCAID-TAN (Aquitania) and in the South GAEL-AG (Gaulacia) or in other words 'The Land of the Gaels of Iber'.

DEMONSTRATION NOTES

WESTERN ASIA

NAMES	EXPLANATIONS
EUPHRATES	**AFFREIDG-EIS**:- Scythian name for the river of sudden impetuous swells or risings.
AR or ARD	**ARD**:- The high land.
AR-MEN-IA	**ARD-MIONN**:- The summit of the Heights of the ERI-MAN.
AR-AR-AT	**AR-ER-AT**:- The high mountain of UR-IANS.
MESOPOTAMIA } **SHINAR**	**MAGH-SEAN-AR**:- Scythian name for 'Plain of the Ancients'. **MAGH-SEAN-AR**:- The land between the two rivers – 'Tigris' and 'Euphrates'.
HIDEKEL	**IAT-DA-CAL**:- 'The Country of the Two Enclosures', the Mesopotamia of the Greeks, the land lying between the rivers 'Tigris' and 'Euphrates'.
ASSHUR	**EISSHOIR**:- Multitudes from the East

'ASHUR-IANS'.

NAMES	EXPLANATIONS
SGADAN	**SIDON or ZIDON**:- Phoenician Port.
AOIMAG	**HAMATH**:- People of Hamath or Syria and Lebanon.
GAAL	Kindred of the same Tribe.
UR	The element of Fire – Light- Brightness.
URAT	**UR-IAT**:- 'The Place of Fire'. The name of all the Chief Places of all the Scythian Tribes that had reference to fire.
URIM And **THUMMIM**	} **UR-IM/ER-IM**:- The perfection of **THETH-IM**:- fire and heat.
BRI-TETHGNE	**GREEK**:- for Fire Mount, pronounced Bri-tinni. Bri, meaning Mount. Tethgne meaning Fire.
BRI-TEGNE **BRI-TEIGNE**	} **GAAL-SCIOT-IBER**:- for Fire Mount, pronounced Bri-tinni.
BREO **CCEAN**	**PHOENICIAN**:- for Fire. **PHOENICIAN**:- for 'Head' – i.e. 'Headland', making **'BREO-CCEAN'** 'Fire Headlands', or 'Chief' – 'Eminent'.

NAMES	EXPLANATIONS
CCEAN-MOR	**'GREAT HEAD'** as in KENMORE, in Scotland.
ASTI	Dwelling (booth) of the Guardian of the Sacred Fires on the Fire Mount.
SILURES	**SUL-UR-EIS**:- 'The Tribe of the Sun and Fire'. (Ancient British Tribe of Wales)
BRIGANTES	**BREO-CCEAN-TIES**:- pronounced Bro-gan-tes 'The Tribe of Breo-ccean' – 'Head Tribes of the Gaels'.
ASTI-ER-EIS	Great Congregation
BRI-TEIN-OL	Great Congregation
BRI-TEGENOL	Great Congregation
BRI-TEGNE	Small Congregations, or Fire Mounts.
DEAS	Represents SOUTH, when facing EAST, **DEAS** was the original name given by the Gaal-Sciot-Iber for Southern Ireland, which became **MUMAIN** or **MUNSTER**.
COLBA	To this day the Haven of the River **BOYNE** is called **IMBAR COLBA** from **COLBA**, the Iber Prince, who drowned when the Gaal-Sciot-Iber invaded

Ireland 1007 BC.

BEOLRAD-FEINE   Scythian written Language

GREAT-BEOLRAD   Scythian unwritten Language

CENCUS   **CEAN-SEIS**:- The Heads of the multitudes.

CIN-CIN-A-TUS   **CEAN-CEAN-IAT-EIS**:- The Head, over the Head of the People.

ARD or AR   High Summit

ARD-BRACCAN   **ARD-BREACAN**:- Place of great slaughter. The <u>heap</u> of the party coloured – because there were laid beneath it men of all the Nations of Eri.

TAN   District or County.

SENATORES   **SEAN-ATHAIR-AOS**:- Followship of the Old Fathers.

MAG-SEAN-ATAIN   Pronounced **MA-SENAR**:- The Plains of the Old Fathers.

BAN-GOR   **BAN-COR**:- Hill of Dance and Music.

INNIS   **I-NIS**:- An Island. Ireland's Poetic name is **'INNIS-FAIL'** – meaning 'Isle of

Destiny'!! INNIS-FAIL, being derived from FAUL or LIA-FAIL, the Stone of Destiny. Jacob's Pillar Stone, which was brought to Ireland by JEREMIAH and set up at TARA, and upon which all the Kings were crowned.
ENCYCLOPEDIA BRITANNICA ELEVENTH EDITION VOL. 14 PAGE 569.

CIER — Son of Eocaid – drowned on arrival in Ireland. The heap of CIER is near KENMARE river.

CORY BANTES — **COR-BEIN-AOS**:- A brotherhood famous for music.

ISLE OF MAN — **IM-AON-AR**

CASSITERIDES — **CASAN-TUR-EIDER**:- A path between the land.

FLAMBOROUGH-HEAD — **BREO-CEAN**:- Flame Head.

GIBRALTAR — **GIOBUR-AILT-ARD**:- The ragged high fire cliffs.

CHAPTER SIX

The Spanish Connection
Part Three
The Writings of Eolus

Names of the Chiefs Who Ruled the Gaal of Sciot in Galicia of Spain From 1491 to 1007 BC

CALMA . . . . .15 YEARS

RONARD . . . . .17 YEARS

DUIL. . . . . .31 YEARS

NINE HEADS OF THE PEOPLE. . . . . .25 YEARS

ENAR. . . . . .35 YEARS

EOLUS. . . . . .33 YEARS

DON. . . . .67 YEARS

LUGAD . . . . .11 YEARS

CEAN-MOR . . . . .17 YEARS

CEAN-ARD. . . . . .20 YEARS

MARCAH . . . . .16 YEARS

CUIR. . . . . .20 YEARS

AOD. . . . . .22 YEARS

IBER . . . . .4 YEARS

MAOL . . . . .18 YEARS

IBER . . . . .23 YEARS

MARCAD . . . . .33 YEARS

NOID . . . . .19 YEARS

OG . . . . .21 YEARS

ARDFEAR . . . . .15 YEARS

BILL . . . . .5 YEARS

EOCAID . . . . .17 YEARS

Once again the Genealogy of the 'Chiefs' of the 'Gaal-Sciot-Iber' have been given above for the reader to follow the narrative.

Much the same as in Ireland, and in Spain (Eis-Feine), and Gaul-atia between the years 1490 BC to 1000 BC we have various groups of settlers.

1.   A COLONY OF ZARAH/CALCOL DESCENDANTS OF JUDAH-ISRAEL.

2.   THE SHEMETIC SCYTHIANS. THE GAAL SCIOT OF IBER.

3.   THE SCYTHIAN BRYTHONS OF BASQUES.

4.   THE CANAANITE PHOENICIANS

5.   A SMALL SCATTERING OF OTHER SETTLERS OF SIMILAR BLOODSTOCK.

} EIS-FEINE-ISH

Just as in Ireland – the Colonies, descendants of ZARAH/CALCOL, BRYTHONS, and GAAL-SCIOT-IBER, being out of the same bloodstock of Hebrews, integrated into one community, but with separate leaders, due to their common Shemetic Ancestry. On the other hand, much the same as in Ireland, the Canaanite Phoenicians from SIDON and HAMATH developed into a separate community, and again much as in Ireland, were a continual source of trouble with devious dealings and much injustice towards the other settlers in the land.

A Synopsis of the Reign of Chiefs of the Gael-ag –

Calma to Eolus 1491 – 1335 BC

CALMA ruled over the Gaal (people) of Sciot in Gael-ag for fifteen years, when he died he was much lamented by his people. DUIL, his son, was but a youth. The Gaal accepted no ruler under twenty five years of age so RONARD, the brother of CALMA, was chosen to succeed him. Ronard ruled for seventeen years.

Duil, the son of Calma, eventually became Chief. Before this he had journeyed back to the land of his Fathers and taken for his wife the daughter of an Uncle – another brother of his Father Calma. Her name was CARMA, but changed it to SCIOTA. When Duil had ruled for thirty one years there was a great plague in which he, and all who were of the Royal Seed died, save a young Grandson of Duil's, who was not a year old. The Gaal kept him and his nurse in a cave and burned seaweed near continually to keep off the infection. The child's name was ENAR. Nine Heads, or Chiefs ruled the land until Enar became of age, viz. twenty five years. Enar ruled for thirty five years.

His son EOLUS was chosen to succeed him although he was not the eldest (1368 BC).

While his Father yet lived, Eolus had journeyed to Iber, the land of their Fathers, and to the land of AOIMAG (HAMATH in SYRIA) to gain knowledge. He desired also to go to Mesopotamia, but difficulties prevented him. He tarried a full year and was three months in Sgadan (SIDON), where he learned to write under the instruction of Scythian Phoenician Scholars. This was Eolus, the man who collected and wrote these 'Chronicles', which hitherto had been preserved and transmitted orally from Father to Son. He was faithful to write only what he believed to be the truth, as it had been passed down from Father to Son, while living in their tents in patriarchal conditions where the Father controlled and led his own family in their simple religion. They worshipped God, looking upon the Sun as His Personification – under the name of BAAL. Eolus wrote down a code of Moral Laws, which in tone agree remarkably with the Commandments given to Moses at Sinai. It must be pointed out that the events being recorded here were conterminous with the events surrounding the Exodus of the Twelve Tribes of Israel from Egypt and the events in Sinai 1491 BC.

The Laws codified by Eolus are given in Chapter VI of Volume 1 'THE WRITINGS OF EOLUS'.

I have included the whole of this Chapter – it is one of the most moving in the whole of the 'Chronicles'. This is Eolus's farewell to his people:-

Chapter VI

THE REIGN OF EOLUS. THIS IS HE WHO WROTE ALL THE FOREGOING TRADITIONS OF HIS RACE, AND NOW SPEAKS OF HIS OWN TIMES, A SPACE OF ONE SCORE AND THIRTEEN RINGS, FROM 1368 TO 1335 BEFORE CHRIST.

THE WRITING OF EOLUS

Now Dalta, the first born of Enar, was not chosen, Eolus was placed on the seat of his Father.

And Eolus, before he was chosen, whilst his father yet lived, had journeyed to Ib-er of our fathers, and to the land of Aoimag, to get knowledge; and his wish was to go even unto Mag-sean-ar,(a) the abode of our great fathers, but the difficulties were greater than his desire.

And Eolus tarried one entire ring, and one Ratha(b) in Sgadan, where he hath learned to set down all his thoughts in shapes and figures, for the eye of man.

I am that Eolus, the son of Enar, the son of Airt, of the race of Calma, from Ardfear, <u>who write down these records, for the instruction of those that now be, and of those who are yet to come.</u>

<u>To teach man to rule himself</u>, that his reason may keep his passions in subjection continually, to tell to the chiefs, and the heads of the Gaal, and to the Gaal of their race, the renowned of the earth.

And these words have I written, as they have been repeated from mouth to ear, from generation to generation, and these times have I noted from the marks of the rings of Baal, and these words are true, according to the traditions of man as believed; but more correct are the times, being according to the revolutions of Baal, which cannot err.

But I, Eolus, have not set down the words said by the Priests, to have been delivered to the nine Priests by Baal, from the beginning, because my understanding cannot give entertainment thereunto; my senses admit not the belief that Baal hath at any time held talk with one of the children of this earth.

Afore priests were, have we not heard of the words spoken by the fathers to their children, as they listened to their voice, beneath the covering of the tents, each of his dwelling, ere the congregations were gathered together, round the habitations of the priests. (bb)

Then did each father declare unto those descended from his loins.

1. Give praise and thanks to Baal, the author of light and life.

2. Shed not the blood of thy fellow, without just cause.

3. Take not aught belonging unto another secretly.

4. Keep falsehood from thy lips – falsehood perverts justice.

5. Keep envy from thy heart – envy corrodes the spirit.

6. Keep flattery from thy tongue – flattery blinds the judgement.

7. Pay respect to thy father, conform thyself unto his will, be thou a sure prop to his old age.

8. *Love, honour, and cherish thy mother, let thy hand wait on her eye – thy foot move in obedience to her voice; for the first pain that you causest to her, she was quit for the joy at thy coming forth, beware of bringing grief to thy mother's heart, the thought will sting thy spirit in the time to come.*

9. *Contend not with thy brother – unity becometh brethren.*

10. *Be loving and protecting unto thy sister.*

11. *Cherish the widow, nourish the orphan, deprived of his father, his staff, never more to hear a tender mother's voice.*

12. *Relieve the poor, the needy, and distressed, be kind, and minister unto the stranger far from the dwelling of his kindred.*

13. *Be merciful to every living creature.*

14. *Be watchful to keep thy passions in obedience to thy reason, in the first place, thereby wilt thou avoid doing unto another, what thou wouldst not have another do unto thee.*

15. *Preserve the glory of thy race, die or live free. (c)*

<u>*What have these things to do with feeding fires, and looking after portions of the land.*</u>

And when Eolus had ruled nine rings he placed Dalta his brother in his seat, and he did go to Sgadan, and he did abide there for one ring, and he did make a covenant with Ramah, chief of the land of Aoimag.

And Ramah did send Olam to abide amongst the Gaal in Gael-ag, and the teachers of Aoimag did give knowledge unto the nobles instructing them to hold talk one with another, from the land of Aoimag even unto Gael-ag.

Moreover men of Aoimag taught the Gael to form ships, wherein to move on the face of the deep.

And the Gael do help the children of Feine; in the bowels of the earth, in the land of Eisfeine, for the children of Ib-er were cunning workmen in the land of their fathers, in searching for brass. (d)

And Eolus did send nine of the sons of Ib-er, even the most wise of the children of the land, to make addition to the knowledge they had aforetime.

And the men did return at the set time of three rings, and Eolus called together the chiefs of the Gael, to the great congregation, (e) and he spake unto them saying,

'Man differeth nothing from the beast of the field, save in reason, but whereto serveth reason, if it receiveth not a right direction?'

'Hath man passions in common with all other animals, which oft consume him, reason instructed will control them.'

'Teachers are now amongst us – what if a portion of the land were assigned to each of Olam in divers quarters, that they may live free from care, save that of instructing the youth in the ways of knowledge – Gael-ag hath hitherto contained too few of the wise men of the earth.'

And it was so –

And the Olam had their portions, and they did choose from amongst them one; Tarlat the son of Leir, to be Ard-olam.

And Tarlat sware in the presence of the congregation to guard the writing, which Eolus did place within his hands, to set down words of the Gaal, to keep falsehood therefrom, and to preserve them during his days.

Now when Eolus had ruled for the course of eighteen rings, it came to pass that Ramah, chief of the children of the land of Aoimag died, and Amram his brother's son took his place. (f)

And Amram sent letters unto Eolus – in this wise, 'The children of Iber within Eis-feine have neglected to pay their tribute. Doth Eolus desire that servants of Amram should go thither, rather than that Eolus send his servants therewith to Sgadan – so be it.'

And Eolus called together all the chiefs, and of the heads of the people, one from every ninth of the tents of Gael.

And Tarlat was in his place, and he read aloud the words of Amram, whereupon a loud murmur ran through the congregation:

And when the air was still, Eolus rose in the midst, and he did put into the hands of Tarlat, words for Amram, and these are they:

'Eolus the son of Enar from Calma of the race of Ard-fear, chief of the Gael of Sciot of Iber, within Gael-ag unto Amram, chief of Aoimag, "Seven score rings and one have been marked since Calma and Ron-ard did hither come with children of the Gael of Sciot of Iber in ships of Feine, for a price fixed, and paid, from which time to this, we have lived free, no mention made of tribute all these days.

Have we not this land from our fathers, and shall we not so leave it to our children? <u>Gael-ag is not, nor ever was Eisfeine</u>.

When Lonrac thought to put Ib-er under tribute, did not File answer

> 'The men of Ib-er will no tribute pay,
>
> Should Lonrac hither come,
>
> The way is far, and perhaps...'

So answereth Eolus, and the host of Gael-ag now.'

And the words were good.

And the servant of Amram, with the words of Eolus, and Morlat a chief of Gael-ag, took their departure for Aoi-mag.

And Morlat returned in due season, with letters from Amram, saying,

'Eidar, servant of Amram, hath erred, the letters of tribute were for Meorl, chief of the children of Ib-er in Buas-ce.'

Now messengers came from Meorl unto Eolus, saying, 'Amram of Aoi-mag demandeth tribute of us. <u>The children of Feine are covetous, they are deceitful</u>; should we submit unto them, short time will pass, till the Gaal of Sciot will be afflicted.

Let the men of Ib-er, Naoimaideis, Oigeageis, be all of one mind, neither Amram, not all nations of the earth, will be able to trouble them.'

And Eolus answered and said, 'Doth a covenant stand between you and them?'

And the messenger answered, 'Yea, to help them on the face of the deep, and in the bowels of the earth within Eis-Feine.'

And Eolus said, 'Have ye observed these things?' And the messenger answered, 'Yea.'

And Eolus said, 'Return to the tents of thy dwellings, and let all the children of all the Gaal of Ib-er be as one man, to resist the oppressor, to live free, or perish.'

And Amram stirred up the nations, their servants on the far side Duor against Gael-ag, but they were slow to move.

And the servants of Amram sought occasions to vex the children of the land of Buas-ce, but after a while they ceased.

And the Gaal are become of renown – they increase in number, and in knowledge continually.

Eolus saith unto the Olam, 'Nourish the minds of the youth, let the glory of Eolus be to leave his spirit amongst the children of the earth, after the grossness of which his bulk is composed shall become part of other substance – or nought – if so be.'

And when Eolus had ruled one score and thirteen rings, he felt himself feeble, like unto the weakness of one about to cease, and he sent for his son Don, and for me Tarlat.

<u>And unto Don he said</u>, 'If thou shalt be chosen to sit in the place of thy father, be thou, and instruct the Gaal to beware of the devices of the children of Feine, they are covetous, they are deceitful, with their lips they give honour to Baal, in works they have respect for riches only.

<u>My son</u> – Make use of thy understanding, learn to depend on thy senses – give not credit to the words thy ear heareth, till thou shalt have examined them thoroughly, and be assured reason hath directed thy judgement; above all, that vanity of thy own opinion had no part therein.

If thou wilt lay up in thy heart the words that thy father hath set down, they will be treasure, from which thou wilt draw profit continually, and thereby wilt thou experience felicity in the first degree.'

<u>And turning unto me, Tarlat</u>, he said, 'Tarlat, nourish the spirit of the youth, guard the writings of Eolus, preserve the chronicles of thy days, keep falsehood therefrom, teach the children of Gael-ag to practise virtue, and they will be happy.'

And these were the last of the words of Eolus heard by me, Tarlat. Eolus, the wisest of the sons of Ib-er, his spirit will abide forever amongst men, who delight in good, and would shun evil.

And all the children of the land mourned for Eolus, calling him father, and instructor.

Notes of Chapter IV

(a)   Look at the Dissertation and Glossary.

(b)   Ratha means an arch, one quarter of a ring.

(bb)   The word in the original is 'asti', as explained in the Dissertation.

(c)   This was the primitive doctrine, before morality was disfigured by impostures and superstition, it forcibly inculcates the practice of virtue, exhibited in its native simplicity and loveliness; would to heaven it had been suffered to abide.

(d)   This is confirmed by Ezekiel, in fact the Hebrews called a miner Ib-er.

(e)   Britelgneol, in the original means the great congregation - look at the Dissertation.

(f)   Every line of this history proves the intimacy that subsisted between this tribe and Sydon. You will bear in mind that the government of Sydon always spoke of Gael-ag and Buasce as if they belonged to, and were a part of Eisfeine, but that the Gaal of both lands would not admit it.

To the eighteenth year of Eolus, the writing was his work; henceforward the history is the compilation of the writings of the several Ard Olam of Gael-ag and Ullad in Eri.

In the language of Eri, Eolus means wisdom; whether he had his name from his superior understanding, or wisdom hath been called Eolus from this, I cannot determine; be it as it may, he was a man of rare endowments.

Priestcraft and Priesthood

After the Gaal of Sciot had settled in GAEL-AG (GAULACIA), they seem to have had 'Priests' come among them, who gradually became a source of trouble and mischief. Eolus does not inform us from where they came, but I suspect that they were of Canaanite origin. Eolus was very wary and watchful against them.

When he had ruled nine years, he placed his brother in his seat to rule while he returned to SGADAN (SIDON), where he stayed for one year. While there, he made a covenant with RAMAH, Chief of the Land of Aoimag (Phoenicians), and Ramah sent 'OLAM' (teachers) to live among the Gaal of Sciot to give them knowledge, and to instruct the Nobles to hold communication between the Lands of Aoimag and Gaelag; also the men of Aoimag taught them to build ships.

The Gaal of Sciot joined the other settlers in their mining operations, as 'the children of Iber were cunning workmen in the land of their fathers, searching for brass'.

According to O'Connor, it is confirmed by Ezekiel, that the Hebrews called a miner, 'Ib-er' (Volume 1 pp 38).

That the word 'Sgadan' – means, in the language of Eri, the Fish Herring, called by the translators of the Bible 'ZIDON', and by the Romans SYDON ...... and other Ancients, because of the immense quantity of fish that frequented that quarter, and the only shoals of fish that are known to come in shoals nigh unto the shore, are herring, pilchards, and sprats! (Volume 1 pp 28)

Now this seems to indicate that ZIDON or the ZIDON-ITES were of the tribe of ZEBULON (GENESIS 49: 13) whose descendants in this day seem to be the people of HOLLAND or 'ZEALAND' – i.e. 'ZEBUL-LAND' – The 'Dutch' being the inventors of herring fishing and the curing of herring! And amongst the leading Seafaring Nations on the Earth.

So in all probability these are the people to whom Eolus contacted on his return to Sgadan! – 'The Zebulonites'.

It is also recorded – and the Gael do help the children of Fein in the bowels of the earth, in the land of Eis-Feine. To this O'Connor adds – 'SPAIN was colonized by people called Feine-cis and is spelled in the original

'EIS-FEINE-AITH', which means 'The Land of the Tribe of Husbandmen'. He writes that:- Though the Government of Sidon (Phoenicia) strove to establish the name EIS-FEINE (Land of Phoenicians) to the area, the attempt was always resisted by the Iberians, who persisted in distinguishing their lands as GAEL-AG and BUASCE. Does this account for the BASQUES resistance toward being classified as SPAN-ISH (EISFEINE-ISH) today!

Phoenicians and the Tribe of Gad

For more than 500 years up to the time of Eolus – the Phoenicians had established a Port at <u>GAD</u>-ES (later known as CADIZ).

The word <u>GAD</u> being the name of another of Israel's Tribes <u>thus showing the depth to which the various tribes of Israel had become integrated with Phoenician trading activities</u>. GAD-ES became the hub of trade for them, chiefly in precious metals. Pioneers in the Mining Industry in Spain, had been the Industrious Celts, who from Ancient Times in their Homeland of AR-MEN-IA had sought for, and mined gold, silver, and copper, to use in their unique Celtic Crafts.

Priesthood

After Eolus returned from Sidon – he sent nine of the wisest of his young men to travel back to SIDON and the lands of their fathers in ARMENIA to gain further knowledge in addition to that which they had already received. They returned after three years. Eolus gave them portions of the land, and placed them as teachers among the people. They were called OLAM, and one was chosen to be ARD-OLAM (the word ARD in Hebrew meaning High or Eminent) – High Priest. TARLAT was chosen to be the first ARD-OLAM.

To him Eolus gave the writings which he had made, and Tarlat sware in the presence of the BRITELGNEOL (Congregation) 'TO GUARD THE WRITING, TO SET DOWN WORDS OF THE GAEL, TO KEEP FALSHOOD THEREFROM, AND TO PRESERVE THEM DURING HIS DAYS'.

After this time, all the writing of the 'Chronicles' was the work of the ARD-OLAM.

When Eolus had ruled for one score and thirteen 'rings', he became ill, and knew that he was about to die. He sent for his son, Don, and Tarlat, and made his last farewell to them. Eolus departed this life 1335 BC.

Do read the words of Eolus to his son, Don and Tarlat again before proceeding.

The Beacon Fires

Before <u>we</u> say farewell to Eolus there is just one further statement which he made which seems at first glance to be rather curious indeed, and requires an explanation. Just <u>after</u> giving the laws, 'as they have been repeated from mouth to ear, from generation to generation', he says:-

> *'WHAT HAVE THESE THINGS TO DO WITH <u>'FEEDING FIRES'</u> AND LOOKING AFTER PORTIONS OF THE LAND'.*

(Volume 1 pp 32)

What a strange statement indeed – it comes right out of the blue – (just like the statement made by Isaiah in our Theme Verse) ISAIAH 24: 14-16.

Just like Isaiah – Eolus made the remark to people who knew what was meant by it – he, like Isaiah, did not consider it necessary to explain what he meant so that future generations would understand.

Yes indeed! – what does the **<u>feeding of fires</u>** have to do with the laws and **<u>looking after portions of the land</u>**.

During their stay in Galicia the SCIOT had learned the craft of shipbuilding. By the time of Eolus, both they, and the Phoenicians, had sizable fleets. Although it seems that the Phoenicians had restricted the size of the ships of the Gaal of Sciot Iber to those comparable to a Modern Fishing Trawler. During the rule of DON, son of Eolus, the boats of the SCIOT were only allowed to 'float on the deep, not farther than one days distance from the land'.

Not only did the Phoenicians have large ships on the Oceans – but other Nations also, including those of the tribe of DAN and ZEBULUN. Many ships passed the Coasts of Eis-Feine and Gael-ag on their commercial journeys. Any seaman will tell you how treacherous that Coast is for sudden squalls and violent storms, especially around Cape Finnistere, and in the Bay of Biscay, many ships were blown onto, or sailed too close to the promontories and outcrops, and were sunk with much loss of life.

The OLAM had for some time been concerned about this. So to warn shipping they had built a series of BEACON FIRES all along the Headlands, which they tended on a Rota System each night, and also during times of bad weather. It must have been an impressive sight for passing ships crews.

According to Dr O'Connor, all the headlands and promontories --belonging to the Gaal of Sciot on the North Western Coast of Spain were called in the Phoenician Language 'BREOCCEAN', that is, 'THE LAND OF FLAMING FIRES'! 'BREO' meaning:- Fires, pronounced BRI/BREE, 'CCEAN' meaning:- eminent, pronounced KEN.

Therefore, what Eolus was saying to the OLAM was, it is a good cause that you have undertaken, but in doing so do not neglect your duty in seeing that the people keep these Laws, they are just as important as keeping the Fires. In keeping these Laws you **'save the souls'** of your fellow men.

'And in the keeping of them the <u>Nation</u> will not perish...' 'If thou wilt lay up in thy heart the words that thy father hath set down, they will be a treasure, from which thou wilt draw profit continually, and thereby wilt thou experience felicity in the first degree.'

Of course this partially answers the theme verse from Isaiah Chapter 24: <u>I say partially</u> answers because, in that Scripture, Isaiah's message is to 'the isles of the sea'. Spain is not an island, neither is it the 'uttermost part of the earth'. At one time it is considered to be so, and the most Westerly Promontory was called by the early settlers and Romans 'Cape Finnis-terra' (End of the Earth). But Spain does not fulfil the requirement of being **'the Isles of the Sea, at the uttermost <u>part</u> of the earth'**, therefore we must look for another piece of the jigsaw to give us the answer to this curious statement by Isaiah.

THE CHRONICLES OF GAEL-AG

A Synopsis of the Reign of the Chiefs of Gael-ag –

Don to Eocaid 1335 BC – 1008 BC

The reign of Don, the son of Eolus, a space of three score rings, from 1335 to 1268 BC.

The Chapter commences:- **'And Don was chosen in the place of his father, and he had ships made by the men of Gael-ag, and he delighted to go therein on the great sea. And many of the Gaal perished in the ships, which the waves of the waters overbore to the earth beneath, Alas.'**

When Don had ruled for eleven rings, TARLAT died, and LOTAR was chosen ARD-OLAM.

During his rule, the Chief of the Aoimag allowed much injustice to be done to the men of Iber who worked the mines in Eis-Feine, keeping them as captives. Don would have settled the matter by battle, but his counsellors prevailed upon him to send first and enquire. Messengers were sent to and fro, and a covenant was made that the Gaal in the mines should have Overseers of their own race, and be sure of returning to their own land when their engagements expired. After this, the Chief of the Aoimag demanded tribute from the Gaal for floating their ships on the sea. The Gaal were of one mind, they refused to pay tribute, and withdrew their vessels into the mouths of the rivers. After some time the Chief of the Aoimag sent to tempt more of the men of Iber to work in the mines, and he would allow the ships of Gael-ag of a certain size to float on the deep, not farther than one days distance from the land. <u>So great was the desire of DON for his ships, he besought the chiefs to have it so</u>. As DON was very aged, they consented to his wish. DON died aged ninety three years, and ruled sixty seven thereof.

During the reign of DON there were four replacements to the office of ARD-OLAM.

TARLAT   First ARD-OLAM in the days of EOLUS.

LOTAR   In the days of DON.

FOR   In the days of DON.

MIN   In the days of DON.

FOIRNAR   In the days of DON.

<u>LUGAD</u>, a grandson of DON was chosen to succeed him. He was skilled in Astronomy, and in the Action of the Sea and Rivers, Oceanography and Cartography. When he had ruled eleven years, he placed CEAN-MOR, his brother, in his seat, and chose three of the OLAM to accompany him to RUAD-AIT (Red Country – Edom) for he had heard great things of the wise men of that land, but the country was swept with pestilence, and they perished. CEAN-MOR continued to rule. He ruled with wisdom and justice for seventeen years, in peace and prosperity, and the Gaal increased exceedingly. During his days TOIRNAR and DOL became ARD-OLAM.

O'Connor informs us that CEAN-MOR means:- Great Head, it is called in Modern Times 'KENMORE' by the Scots.

<u>CEAN-ARD</u>, the youngest of the sons of LUGAD, succeeded him. Eocaid, his brother was angry that he had been superceded and tried to rouse the Gaal against Cean-ard; those who held with Eocaid left Gael-ag and passed over the Pyrenees and dwelt on the other side, calling the land Eocaid-tan (AQUITANIA) (SEE DEMONSTRATION NOTES).

When Cean-ard had ruled twelve years, a sore famine oppressed Gael-ag, greatly reducing the number of the people and their cattle. During his days GOL succeeded as Ard-Olam.

MARCAH, his son succeeded Cean-ard. After a rule of sixteen years he was thrown from his horse and killed while hunting deer. (This is the first mention of the horse, or of hunting in the 'Chronicles'). The Olam ends his obituary by saying – 'Oh! how afflicting to behold the thin congregations, as they stand feebly round the Mounds!'

CUIR, the brother of Marcah was chosen to succeed him. He was a lover of the chase and all manner of sports. He sent many youths to the land of Aoimag to learn the harp. He took more delight in these things than in the teaching of the Olam. He died after a rule of nineteen years.

AOD, the son of Marcah was chosen. During his days 'Naught was heard through Gael-ag but the sound of the harp, the song, naught is seen but folly, and the dance'. After a rule of twenty two years Aod died.

IBER, the son of Aod reigned for four years, he was killed by FALB, a Chief of the Gael-ag whose wife Iber had taken. During his days MOLT was chosen Ard-Olam.

MAOL, the brother of Iber was chosen to succeed him. In his time the 'Priests' gained great influence in the land, and extorted 'offerings' from the people. Maol gave the 'Priests' authority to elect for themselves a Chief Priest, under the Title of ARD-CRUIMTIER. Maol died after a rule of seventeen years.

The 'Priesthood' had gained ascendancy, for a long while they were jealous of the Olam, from this time they became a great source of trouble to the people. During his days NER became Ard-Olam.

IBER, the son of Maol was chosen. He ruled entirely under the influence of the Priests, and the people paid little attention to the teachings of the Olam – (much the same as today) – NER stating, **'the youth do not flock to the 'Booths' of the Olam, as aforetime.'** Iber ruled for twenty three 'rings'.

<u>MARCAD</u>, his son succeeded Iber, **'his days were spent in idleness, and was directed in all matters by the Priests'.** During his days NER died and SULARD was chosen as Ard-Olam. He died after a rule of thirty three years.

<u>NOID</u>, was chosen to succeed his father, he died after a rule of nineteen years.

<u>OG</u>, the youngest brother of MARCAD was chosen. After a rule of four years SULARD died and FEILIMID was chosen Ard-Olam. Also at this time multitudes of the Gaal, with many of the Heads of the People, led by a great-grandson of the Chief FALB, who slew King Iber, passed over the Pyrenees, where some of their race had gone before, to escape the oppression and greed of the 'Priests' who seemed to have all the rule in Gael-ag. When OG had ruled for twenty years, multitudes from the lands of Aoimag entered Spain because of the troubles in their own land. The Gaal of Sciot received them and treated them with kindness, remembering that they had received all their increase of knowledge from that land. They brought with them yet more knowledge of music and dancing but the 'Chronicles' say:- **'Deceit and treachery are in the men of Aoimag'.** OG died after a rule of twenty one years, **'greatly lamented by the Priests, and them only'**, (According to O'Connor, this period was the time when King DAVID ruled in Israel, and the refugees who entered Spain were from the Philistines and other Canaanite Groups, who fled from his power).

When the Chiefs came together to choose Og's successor many of the 'Priests', with their servants and a great multitude of the Gaal, gathered with them at '<u>THE MOUNT OF ASSEMBLY</u>' and ARDFEAR the son of OG was chosen. When the Ard-Olam Feilimid (as was the custom) attempted to read the 'Writings of Eolus' and the 'Chronicles', many voices were shouting "Down with the Olam! We will not incline our ears to the 'Writings of Eolus'". Then the Ard-Olam hastened and stood by the side of Ardfear, and spoke aloud to the King, the Princes, and Nobles, and the people, reminding them that from the time of Eolus it had been the duty of the Ard-Olam to preserve the 'Writings', even at the risk of his life, to suffer no falsehood to be written into the 'Chronicles', and, when a new Chief was chosen to rule, to read the

'Writings' and 'Chronicles' in the hearing of the great congregation there for the occasion. When he had made an end of his exhortation, the people shouted as with one voice (excepting the 'Priests' who had departed from the Mount), **'Let the words be read and heard!'**

After this, a great feast was prepared and spread for all. Soon after this, the Ard-Olam approached the King with the 'Writings' and 'Chronicles' in his hand, and asked him to take them and guard them, **'<u>For they were more precious to the race than all the riches within the bowels of the earth</u>'**. Ardfear asked of whom was he afraid, and was amazed when the Ard-Olam answered, **'Of the Priests'**, but Ardfear promised that he would guard them in a place which the Ard-Olam alone should know. The King cherished the Olam, and the youth crowded the schools, and truth, wisdom and knowledge were sought after.

When Ardfear had ruled eight years, the Priests had so increased in numbers, greed and arrogance, especially since many other Priests from Aoimag had joined them – that Ardfear called together the great congregation, and two Princes, together with the Ard-Olam, were appointed to search out the numbers and condition of the Priests and their servants. This done, the great congregation was again assembled. It was decided that the number of 'Priests' be restricted to **'Nine times nine Priests throughout the land'**, - (i.e. 729).

Provision was to be made for their sustenance – and they were ordered to cease from collecting 'offerings'. The Priests did not like this one bit, and their minds were evil towards Ardfear, so **'They loaded his name with evil report'**, but Ardfear was respected by the Gaal.

At this time multitudes from the land of Aoimag poured into Eis-Feine, and many ships passed by the Coasts of Gael-ag, and messengers came from Sidon to Gael-ag and Buasce. Many of the Gaal entered into the ships of Feine belonging to the Canaanite Phoenicians and went Northward to a strange land, where they entered and abode, '<u>and the merchants brought tin, lead, copper and other precious things from the mines</u>'. The land they went to was the Island of Britain and settled mostly in the area known today as Cornwall and Devon.

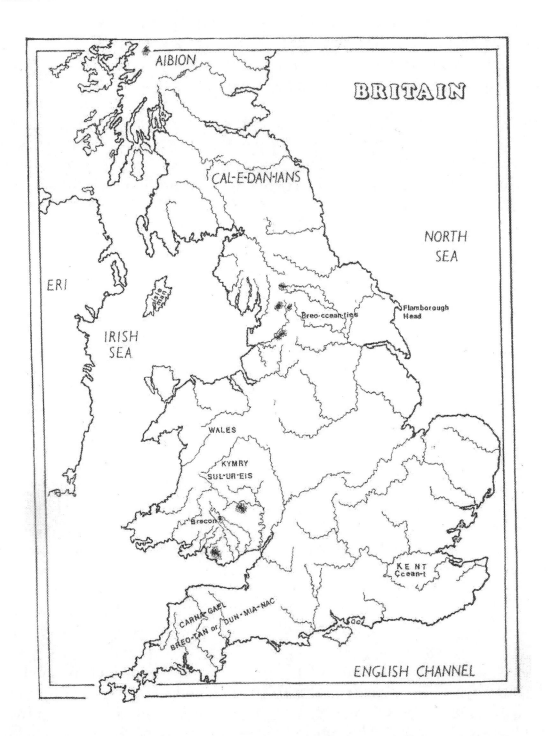

Fig. 11: Map of Britain

CHAPTER SEVEN

The British Connection
The First Migrants of Gaal Sciot of Iber to Britain

It is distinctly recorded in the 'Chronicles' of Gael-ag that in the eighth year of ARDFEAR, Chief of the Gaal-Sciot-Iber, corresponding with the year <u>1037 before Christ</u>, multitudes from Phoenicia passed by <u>BREO-CCEAN</u>, (the general name of all the Headlands of Galicia looking over the ocean) and steered Northward to a strange land which they had previously discovered, the bowels of which they commenced to explore, and from whence they carried off stores of riches, hidden afore time in the caverns of the earth.

That shortly afterwards the Phoenicians recruited miners and labourers from among the Gaal-Sciot-Iber in Gael-ag and Buas-ce, and entered into a covenant with them, in consequence whereof many of the Gael-ag and Basques went to work the Phoenician mines in Britain – locating Tin, Copper and Lead.

The Phoenicians called the island <u>BREO-TAN</u> and the area of Cornwall and Devon 'DUN-MIANAC'.

The name Dun-mia-nac meaning 'Hills of mines'.

The name 'Corn-wall' being a derivative of 'Carna-gael', or 'The Cairn of Altars of the Clan', or Tribe, 'Cairn-gael'. The word Cairn or Carn denoting a heap of stones or rocks. Cornwall is, most people know, a very rugged area.

The Phoenicians did not displace the natives of Scythian descent as afore mentioned under the leadership of HU-GADARN, and who by now had grown very numerous, they mingled with them, employed them in their mining activities, and became very influential in the area, and certainly instituted their language to a great degree.

The increase of these strangers within the country of the Scythian Sciot of Iber descent, and more immigrants pouring in from SIDON and SPAIN, made it necessary to extend their limits, many of them in Clans moved Northwards, crossing the Severn Estuary settling in the districts of Wales, known as Glamorgan, Monmouth, Hereford, <u>Brecon</u> and Radnor – mingling with their Scythian cousins who are known as SUL-URIES, changed by the Romans to:- SILURES.

The 'Chronicles' of the Gael-ag do not furnish this information, but from the 'Chronicles of Eri', in Volume Two, we learn distinctly that multitudes of the Gaal-Sciot-Iber, and the Gaal of Iber, within Buasce, were being treated deceitfully and treacherously by their Phoenician-Sidonian Masters, which resulted in many steering Northward in ships, establishing themselves on the Coast opposite IM-AON-AR (known as the Isle of Man). They spread far North and Eastward, extending their jurisdiction over the present districts of the Mersey, Liverpool, Lancaster, Westmoreland, Cumberland (now C-umbria), Yorkshire and Durham, where they are recognized by their Ancient Iberian name of <u>BREO-CCEAN-TIES</u>, changed by the Romans to BRIGANTES.

BREO being pronounced 'BREE', CCEAN pronounced 'KEN' = BREE-KEN-TIES.

When Ardfear, Chief of the Gael-ag had ruled 'fourteen rings', we are informed in the 'Chronicles' that there was an earthquake, or some disturbance accompanied by a storm, **'And the waters of the deep deluged BREO-TAN (BREE-TAN) and tore a passage through, leaving many fragments in the midst of the waters'** (Volume 1 pp 67).

'Passage thro' and **'thro'**, is in the original 'CASAN-TIR-EIDER' (CASSITERIDES), the literal significance of which is **'a path between the**

land'. And the **'fragments separated'**, is in the original 'SCAOILEAD', pronounced 'SCILLY', which means loosing, untying, or separation.

So here we have a definite record and date, <u>1031</u> BC of the separation of the Isles of Scilly from the Mainland. This disturbance also may have had the effect of widening the English Channel. (Ceylon is also a derivative of SCAOILEAD, proving that, that Island was also known to the Phoenicians).

The Northern area of the Island ALBIN or <u>ALBION</u> means:- **'The summits of confused heaps of mountains'**, which aptly describes Cumberland, Westmoreland, Northumberland, and Scotland. ALBION – is the Ancient Name for Britain.

O'Connor informs us:- Now it is an indisputable fact, that on all the Headlands of the Gael-ag, that is Ard-Iber, Fir-ol and Ard-na-gael, and all the promontories looking over the Ocean, it was the custom to kindle fires, and keep them blazing during the darkness of the night, to be the means of directing seafaring ones, and of protecting them from the perils of the great deep. <u>This kind of fire is called in the Language of Phoenicia, 'BREO'</u>, for which reason all the Headlands of the Gael-ag were called BREO-CEAN, in like manner, on the part of this Island (Britain), opposite to Gael-ag, it was necessary to observe the same salutary custom, for the purpose of guiding the Mariners of Phoenicia on their way from BREO-CEAN to the land of their new and profitable acquisition, they gave it the name BREO-TAN, which in their tongue signifies:- **'THE LAND OF THE FLAMING FIRES'**, - or **'ISLAND OF FLAMING FIRES'**, to distinguish it from Breo-cean, their name for Gael-ag.

It is common knowledge that the practice of lighting Beacon Fires in times of Emergency, Invasion or Assembling the People, has been a fact of British History throughout the Centuries. 'THE MOUNTAINS OF THE BRECON BEACONS' in Wales derive their name from BREO-CCEAN. It must be pointed out that about the time that these events were taking place, in the year 1075 BC, following the destruction of TROY, the great grandson of AENEAS - King BRUTUS the Trojan had landed with his followers at TOTNES in DEVON.

So now residing in BRITAIN were various settlers:-

THE EARLY SCYTHIANS   - KYMRI

                                       BRYTHONS

                                       LLOEGRYS

GAAL-SCIOT-IBER

DARDA/ZARAH – JUDAHITES   - TROJANS

PHOENICIANS

VARIOUS OTHERS.

DEMONSTRATION NOTES

NAMES	EXPLANATIONS
SOMERSET	NEW SUMER LAND as opposed to the OLD SUMER LAND in Mesopotamia.
BRECON-BEACONS	'The Hills of the Fire Beacons'.
SILURES	SUL-UR-EIS – 'The Tribe of the Sun and Fire'.
TIN	STAN (Stan was the original word for this Metal – as appears from the preservation of the Roman word STANARIES (STANNUS).
COR	CIRCLE or CHOIR – MUSIC.
PEN-SANSE	BINN-SEAN-CE - 'The Old Headland'.
PEN-Y-BYD	'Top of the World'.
LIZARD	LOIS-ARD – 'The High Fort'.
GLAMORGAN	GLAS-MOR-CEAN - 'The Head of the Green Sea'.

HEREFORD	ERI-FORAS or ERI-FORD – 'The Passage of the Erians'.
NAMES **BRIGANTES**	**EXPLANATIONS** BREO-CCEAN-TES – 'The Tribe of (Yorkshire Celts) Breo-ccean' or 'The Chief of the Fire Tribes.
IRWELL	ER-BAL – 'The Place of Er'.
LIVERPOOL	LEAR-BAAL – 'The Mouth of the Haven'.
MERSEY	MIR-SE – means 'Partition' of the sea.
PEN-I-GENT	BINN-GEINT – The wedge like Summit, or High Summit.
YORK	IB-OR, IBER or CAER-EB-RAUCE meaning:- 'City of the Iberians', near a river.
GALLOWAY	GAEL-ADH-BEATH – pronounced GUAL-AVIA (The Land of the Gaels).
MULL-OF-KANTYRE	MULLAC-CEAN-TIR – 'The Summit of the Headland'.
LOC-LOMAN	LOC-LO-AMAN – 'A Lake'.
EDIN-BOROUGH	DUN-EADEN – 'The Front of the Fortress'.
BREO-TAN	BRI-TAIN – 'Land of Flaming Fires'.

WALES	WAELS = GAELS
FLAMBOROUGH HEAD	Meaning:- 'Headland of the Fires'.
CALEDONIA	CAL-A-DUN – 'Land enclosed among Hills' – 'Land of the Gael and Dan'.
DALRADIA	DAL-RIG-FADA – The portion of the long armed, which was named by EOCAID CAIBRE, the leader of the first colony from Ireland to Albion.
INIS	I-NIS – An Island, as in 'INNIS FAIL' a poetic name for Ireland, meaning 'Island of Destiny'.
ALBIN	ALBION – Summits of confused heaps or heights – The Ancient name for Britain.
ARD	The High Land – The High Place, as in ARD-GAEL now – AR-GYLE – 'The Gael of the Highlands.
ARAN	Coarse Land – not arable.
TAN	A district of a Country – as in Mauri-tan-ia Lusi-tan-ia, Aqui-tan-ia, Britan-ia.
CALDECOTT	CALD-I-SCIOT, The Inclosure of the Sciot.
CALEDONIANS	CALD-I-DON-IANS – The Inclosure of the Danaans.

AQUITANIA

EOCAID-TAN – 'The Land of Eocaid'. Eocaid being the brother of CEAN-ARD, son of LUGAD 1240 BC, who rebelled at the election of his younger brother as Chief of the Gael-ag in Spain, and with some supporters crossed the Pyrenees into what is now France, and settled between the Ocean, the rivers Garonne and Rhone, and the Pyrenean Mountains, calling their new home EOCAID-TAN, from whence went forth a colony, Eastwards, calling themselves GAEL-DUN-SEIS, which later became WAL-DEN-SES.

WALDENSES

As shown above – derived from GAEL-DEN-SES meaning:- 'The Tribe' or 'Gaal of the Hills'.

CHAPTER EIGHT

The Irish Connection

In order to establish the 'Irish Connection' of the Gael-Sciot-Iber, it is necessary for us to return to the final events which take place in Gael-ag in Spain, where Ard-Fear was the ruling Chief. Ardfear ruled for fifteen years, then he died.

1030 – 1025 BC

Ardfear was succeeded by <u>BILLE</u>, the grandson of Marcad, a cousin of Ardfear. During his days complaints came from the Gaal in Dunmianac (Cornwall and Devon), saying that the men of Iber who had gone there to work the mines were prevented by the Phoenician Merchants (mine owners) from returning home.

Ith, the son of Bille, was sent to enquire into the matter. Ith was a long time gone, as his ship on the homeward journey had been driven by the winds and sea towards the West, where they came to another land – (Ireland), and the natives seemed very frightened of them.

Ith had made a covenant with the Phoenician Mine Owners in Dunmianac, and the Gaal of Iber were made free.

Bille was very old when he began to rule, he died after a reign of five years. During his reign Feilimid the Ard-Olam died also and ORDAC was chosen in his place.

<u>1025 – 1008 BC</u>

<u>EOCAID</u>, Bille's son, was chosen to succeed him, with his reign we have the conclusion of the 'Chronicles' of the Gael-ag in Spain.

Under the rule of Bille the 'Priests' had again increased in power and arrogance.

They now agitated for the Priests and the people who had come from Aoimag twenty years before to have the same privileges and freedom in Gael-ag as the Gaal of Iber. When Eocaid found that the Priests were inciting a conspiracy against him, he assembled the Chiefs and Heads of the People, and after consultation, the order was sent forth that all the strangers from Aoimag were to depart from the area within six months. The Priests, and the 'Fillistin' (Philistines) spread themselves through the people of Eisfeine, and stirred them up against the People of Iber, and had entered the land before Eocaid was aware. Eocaid drew his warriors together and drove the invaders from Gael-ag.

The Phoenician Ruler of Eisfeine promised to remit all tribute for seven years to his people, if they would bring the Gaal of Iber under subjection. Eocaid gathered his people together to defend themselves. For six years the Nations around them harassed the Gaal of Iber, even tried to rob them of the ships on the rivers. Eocaid had all the ships worked out of the rivers to the inlets of the sea and put them under the control of Ith, who was Governor of Ferrol, and dwelt there.

Within six months Ith had all the shipping gathered into the Bay of Ferrol, and set watchers on the Coast. Still the Phoenician seamen strove to take them off. Then Ith commanded that, **'The fires on the heights for the guidance of the seamen were not to be lighted unless ordered'.**

After Eocaid had ruled eight years, once again the people of Eisfeine under Phoenician rule poured into the land, there was a great battle in which the Gaal of Iber were victors. The hosts of Iber named Eocaid – 'GOLAM', which means:- (The Mighty Champion). After this the Gael-ag enjoyed peace, and all the brethren of their race on the Biscayan Coast and over the Pyrenees honoured Eocaid, and all made agreement to fight together in the future if any one of their clans were attacked.

Now Eocaid commanded Ith that the Beacon Fires be again lighted.

O'Connor states in his notes Volume 1 pp 79 **'That this Eocaid is in the 'Tales of the Bards' known by the name of Golam, and is also the MILETUS of Latinity Writers of the 15th Centuries, from whom the Irish are ignorantly and absurdly called MILESIANS!'**

He reigned, as you see, for seventeen years from 1025 – 1008 BC, comparable to the reign of David and commencement of the reign of Solomon – Kings of Israel.

The Egyptian Subjugation of Spain and Gael-ag

It was during the 17th year of the reign of Eocaid that a mighty host from the East rushed like a devastating flood across Africa and parts of Europe sweeping all Nations before them. Eocaid and his warriors met them not far from the river Duor in Spain. The battle was fiercely contested by Eocaid, and his Chiefs, and the Gaal, but the numbers of the enemy were overwhelming. Thousands of the Gaal of Iber were killed, and Eocaid, with three of his sons, and many Chiefs also were slain.

All the clans of the Gael-ag and Nations of Eis-feine were conquered, the victor took away the youths as captives and took much booty and cattle. Gael-ag was a desert, and full of mourning. ORDAS, the Ard-Olam, who recorded these things in Eocaid's time of rule, wrote that, **'He would rather have fallen numbered with the dead if only Golam could have been victorious in the battle'.**

Five sons of Eocaid survived the battle, they retrieved the bodies of their father and brothers and raised a great heap (CAIRN) over them, and called the place Arg-iocad, which they hoped would be a memorial forever.

It is an interesting fact of History that at the time that Solomon had ascended the throne of Israel and started laying the foundation of the Temple, the neighbouring Pharaoh of Egypt was making a foray into far away Spain and adding to the glory of the XXIst Dynasty of that land.

At the head of the huge army, including hundreds of chariots drawn by Egyptian horses, he moved across the shores of Africa, Westward to the Gates of Hercules. There he crossed by boat to Gibraltar and began the invasion of the entire Iberia – Hibernian Peninsula.

In the 'Chronicles' of the Gael-ag Volume 1 pp 78/79, we read:-

> *'And the battle was fought in all the plains between Samur and Duor; Eocaid, and all the chiefs, and all the Gaal fought, destroying, like a consuming fire; but what availeth fire against water? Was not the fire of Ib-er extinguished by the stormy waves <u>of the multitudes of Sru-amac</u>?*
>
> *Thousands of Gaal lay on the earth, and Eocaid, O woe! thou fell into the arms of death on that unhappy day, and three sons of Go-lam, and chiefs in heaps lay round the weight of Eocaid.*
>
> *On that day Sru overthrew Ib-er, and all the Nations of Eisfeine, and he took away captive of the youth, and drove away a huge prey of the cattle of the land.'*

Who was this man Sru-amac? In the History Books he is named SHASHANQ, the first of a series of Rulers of the 21st Dynasty. Although he is called Sru in the 'Chronicles', in the footnotes O'Connor refers to him as SESOSTRIS, which is a Greek word for RAMSES. This could very well have applied to the General in Charge of Sru's Army.

Why did Sru-amac come to conquer Spain? The answer lies in the products which came out of **'the bowels of the earth'**, such as gold, silver and tin. Gold and silver were obtainable elsewhere, but tin came in big quantities from the Mines in Spain – <u>and this was the essential alloy which when mixed with copper produced bronze and brass</u>.

For thousands of years the Phoenicians had kept secret their source of tin. The Nation which had enough tin as an alloy were the masters of others because their weapons were more superior. To own Tin Mines was to obtain power! The Pharaohs of Egypt, in time, had learned about the mines of Spain and her rich veins of tin. Sru had built up a huge arsenal of weapons and swift metal wheeled chariots which guaranteed himself victory in battle. He had in mind subduing the whole civilized world in his time as Pharaoh. After conquering Spain, the source of tin, he had in mind next his neighbour, Israel, and then Assyria!

Solomon, in his wisdom, knew that he could not hope to match this powerful Egyptian Pharaoh in battle. Solomon had much gold and much power himself.

Indeed he had secured hundreds of horses from his Egyptian neighbour with Egyptian chariots to match.

In the Bible, that Pharaoh is called **Shishak** and we read of Solomon's strategy in the Bible and also in the 'Historian's History of the World', (Volume 1 pp 173) of how Shishak – a Pharaoh of the XXIst Dynasty, entered early into relations with the Israelitish State, took Gaza for Solomon and gave it to his daughter as a dowry, and also gave refuge to political refugees like Jeroboam and Hadad of Edom to leave a loophole for intervention.

In marrying Shishak's daughter, Solomon also married her Pagan Religion. He allowed her to erect shrines to the Egyptian Gods on the hills surrounding Jerusalem and in doing so, went against the first of the Ten Commandments of Israel's one God! The result was catastrophic! In the Bible we read the account of Shishak's visit to Jerusalem on the way to Assyria. Here is how it goes:-

Shields of Gold for Shields of Brass

> *'And it came to pass in the fifth year of King Rehoboam (who succeeded Solomon after he died), that Shishak, King of Egypt came up against Jerusalem: And he took away the treasures of the King's House; he even took away all: and he took away all the shields of gold which Solomon had made.*

> **And King Rehoboam made in their stead brazen shields, and committed them into the hands of the chief of the guard, which kept the door of the King's house.**

> (1 Kings 14: 25-27)

Solomon's reign has been called, quite properly, the Golden Age of Israel. God had allowed him to complete his forty years of reign. He had allowed him to build and complete the Temple at Jerusalem. And during his lifetime Israel was without question the dominant nation of the earth. The momentum which had begun with David's forty years of rulership was allowed to continue and to build up during Solomon's reign. But Solomon's wives turned his heart away from God.

> **'For it came to pass, when Solomon was old, that his wives turned away his heart after other gods: and his heart was not perfect with the Lord his God, as was the heart of David his Father.**

> (1 Kings 11: 4)

Because of David, God withheld judgement from Solomon. Five years after the death of Solomon, Shishak humbled Israel on his way to Syria, taking the golden shields of Solomon as a sign of his sovereignty and making of Rehoboam a mere vassal. There was a reason, then, why Rehoboam replaced the shields of gold with shields of brass in the palace at Jerusalem.

The Last Days in Gael-ag

MARCAD, son of Eocaid was chosen to succeed his father. The land of Gael-ag was devastated by the terrible battle and to make matters worse there was a great drought in which people, cattle and vegetation perished. Marcad and the other Chiefs met to consider what was to be done. Ith, the 'Sailor Chief of Ferrol', suggested that he take three ships and one hundred and forty youths, and go seek that strange island to the West of Breo-tan which he had seen nineteen years before, and return and guide all the Gaal who would be willing to go there.

The people agreed and Ith departed. Those that remained worked diligently preparing ships and equipment to leave Gael-ag when Ith should return; **'And the fires that looked over the sea were kept blazing, day and night, to direct Ith and his ships back'.**

Eventually, the watchmen reported three ships coming towards the land. The ships cast anchor, and LUGAD, the son of Ith landed, and reported that his Father Ith, had been killed by the people in the 'Isles of the Sea'. When the honours of interment had been rendered, LUGAD gave an account of his Father's death.

When Ith and his Company had found the land which they sought, he left a third part of his men to guard the ships, and ventured into the country with the rest. They found two Distinct Peoples there, a fierce Tribe called 'The Tuatha-de-Danaans', and the 'Firgneat' (aborigines). The 'Firgneat' were more numerous, but were in subjection by the Danaans as slaves.

On the second day they saw a multitude coming towards them with huge clubs in their hands, and the men were very fair.

Ith's Company defended themselves with their <u>bows and arrows</u>. The battle continued for three days, many fell in combat including Ith. His last words to his son were to urge the Gael of Iber to come quickly to the 'Land of Woods' – suitable for settlement.

When Lugad had made an end, all the people swore an oath of vengeance for Ith's blood. Preparations were made quickly throughout Gael-ag, and soon afterwards all who had escaped the calamities of the preceding few years embarked for the New Land, after the Gaal had sojourned four hundred and eighty four years in Gael-ag, i.e. 1491 BC to 1007 BC. (Please note: In 1491 BC the 12 Tribes were just leaving Egypt).

This Ends the Chronicles of Gael-ag

It seems from this account that the 'Firgneat' were descendants of the early SHELAH/CANAANITE settlers in Ireland. 'Firgneat' meaning (natives), and the Tribe of DAN. It must be remembered that there was a strong Colony of ZARAH/CALCOL descendants on the Island also.

By the account given by Lugad, it seems that Ith and his Company had landed on the South East Coast of Ireland, and as the descendants of ZARAH/CALCOL had settled in the North, they would not in all probability have known of the landing made by the Gael-ag and the consequent battle.

Ard-Olams in Gael-ag

RULER	ARD-OLAM
EOLUS	TARLAT first Ard-Olam
DON	LOTAR
DON	FOR
DON	MIN
DON	FOIRNAR
LUGAD	TOIRNAR
LUGAD	DOL
CEAN-ARD	GOL
IBER	MOLT
MAOL	NER
MARCAD	SULARD
OG	FEILIMID
BILLE	ORDAC

CHAPTER NINE

The Invasion and Subjugation of Ireland By the Gaal Sciot of Iber 1007 BC to 7 BC
This Commences the Chronicles of Eri (Volume Two)

THE CHRONICLES OF ERI –

Volume Two Chapter One

'Here commence the annals of Eri. This chapter gives an account of the arrival of the colony from Spain in Eri – their conquest of three quarters of the island – their covenant with the Danan, the former rulers – their division of their own portion into three separate kingdoms – the contention of Iber and Erimionn – the fall of Iber; and the death of Erimionn. The whole embracing the space from 1006 to 1004 before Christ, being two years.

BAAL was favourable until the host came within sight of the land of their vengeance.

Then did he send forth his messengers of air; and they brake the vessels, and scattered them on every side: twelve ships did the servants of the anger of Baal bury beneath the waves of the vast deep.

On that day was Colba overborne at the mouth of a river of the land. (a)

On that day perished Cier within the jaws of an inlet of the sea at the extremity of the world of land.

Howbeit the remainder of the host with difficulty reached the shore with Marcad, Iolar, and Blat, Volume II.

So commences the Chronicles of Eri: Marcad and the hosts of Sciot of Iber had a favourable voyage until they came within sight of the land, and terrible weather overtook them, and twelve vessels were broken up by the sea and lost.

<u>Colba</u>, one of their Chiefs was lost with his ship – as also was Cier, a brother of Marcad, and much beloved by the Gaal. The remainder of the host reached land with difficulty under the leadership of <u>Marcad, Iolar, and Blat</u>, the three surviving sons of Eocaid. Er – the young son of Cier was taken into the care of Marcad. Marcad commanded that three men should abide with each ship, and that all the woman and children should also stay while their brethren went forward to take vengeance for Ith's blood, and lots were cast to decide who should stay with the ships, but all the men and women likewise cried, **'Let none be left, let all die together, or all have glory of those who shed Ith's blood'**. They would not be entreated.

They landed, and they were met by a large force of DANAN and natives who outnumbered them twenty to one. The battle endured long, but very soon the Firgneat took the side of the Sciot, and the Danan fled. On the next day the battle was renewed, and the Danan were overthrown, for their clubs availed not, and also they had lost the support of the natives. On the third day the Chiefs of the land sent messengers with their clubs behind them, and their hands on their breasts as a token of peace.

The Danan brought with them some men of the Gael who, eight years before had been wrecked on the Coast when on their way in a ship from BREO-TAN to GAEL-AG. There was a great joy in meeting some of their own race. They acted as interpreters between the Sciot and the Danan, and a covenant was made that the Danan should withdraw, and take the whole tract of land to the West of the Island, between the river Shannon and the sea. That land was named 'OLDANMACT', now Galway. The truce was kept and there the Danan exercised their own laws for more than a thousand years.

The Danan set up a large stone on the spot where the covenant was made, and the place was called MAGMORTIOMA. This spot is said to be somewhere near what is now DUNDALK.

The tents of the Sciot were set up round about Magmortioma until the Danan had passed over the river into the West of the Island. The natives remained with the Sciot and assisted them in all things and there was a long peace.

The Danan had invaded Ireland two hundred years before, and ruled the natives with rigour, so it is understandable that they would welcome their new found freedom with the Sciot.

In his notes O'Connor states that **'This place (Mag-mor-tioma) is still called by the same name.'**

We are also informed that the Firgneat were called by the Danan, 'CLODEN'. A term of disrespect in the Danan language. Aborigines were called by the Iberians, 'FIRGNEAT' (native), and 'CEGAIL', meaning:- exhaltations from the earth.

(Notes C and D Volume Two pp 12)

We shall therefore, from this point refer to the natives as 'Firgneat'.

After 'three moons', Marcad called a great gathering of the Sciot of Iber, the purpose of which was twofold:-

1. To decide a name for their new home.

2. How they should govern the land.

'ERI': The Official Name

Marcad suggested that their Island home be called ERI meaning the island of the IBER-IANS. It was also decided to divide the land into three portions, each under the rule of one of the sons of EOCAID (GOLAM). This was agreed to. Marcad from this time decided to be called Iber. All the divisions were settled by lot:-

(Marcad) IBER obtained the South West Portion – MUMAIN (MUNSTER).

IOLAR obtained the Eastern Portion – GAELEN (LEINSTER).

ER, son of CIER obtained the Northern Portion – ULLAD (ULSTER).

The FIRGNEAT were allocated the area known as FER-MAN-AH and DONEGAL.

The DANAAN were already allocated in – OLDANMACT (GALWAY and CONNAUGHT).

BLAT, the other son of EOCAID, would not accept a portion as Chief as he had been elected to be the ARD-CRUIMTER, therefore his portion was given to ER, son of CIER.

A small portion of land, now known as CORK, was given to LUGAD, son of ITH.

It must also be remembered that a colony of CALCOL/ZARAH-JUDAH, were already established in the Northern Portion, now called ULSTER, therefore it seems that ER and his 'Clan' were accepted into this Community due to their Kinship.

It also seems that the CANAANITE descendants of SHELAH-JUDAH integrated with the two Tribes of the East and South in GAELEN and MUMAIN – these were probably many of the early 'Firgneat', and other Canaanite settlers of Phoenician origin, they outnumbered the descendants of Iolar and Iber, and were to exercise great influence in the Politics and Religion of those areas over the years, causing great contention with the descendants of ER and CALCOL in Ulster.

Divisions of Eri – 1000 BC to 7 BC

1. TUATHA-DE-DANAAN	CONNAUGHT – GALWAY
	WEST
2. ER and CALCOL/ZARAH JUDAH	ULLAD (ULSTER)
	NORTH
3. IOLAR	GAELEN (LEINSTER)
	EAST
4. IBER	MUMAIN (MUNSTER)
	SOUTH
5. FIRGNEAT	FER-MAN-AGH –
	(Land of the Ferg-man)

It is very remarkable that this division of the land should have continued with so little change for nearly 3,000 years!

* SEE MAP OF ERI

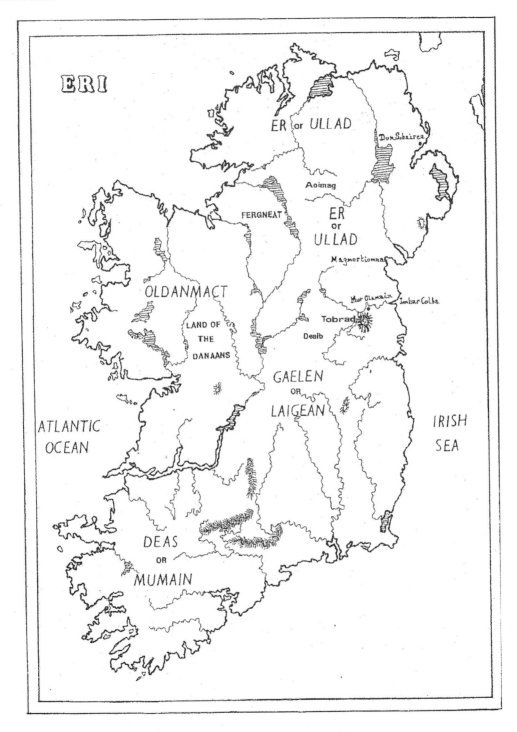

Fig. 12: Map of Eri – (Ire-land)

The Table of Names of the Irish Provincial Kings

From 1000 BC to 700 BC

ULLAD or ULSTER		DEAS
		MUMAIN or MUNSTER
ER . . . . 42 years		IBER . . . . 1 year
IBER . . . . 28 years		ERAC
IBERIC . . . . 34 years		ERNAC
SOBAIRCE . . . . 44 years		CONMAOL
OILLIOL . . . . 24 years		AONGUS
DAIRE . . . . 17 years		CIERMNA
EOCAID . . . . 16 years		AIRT
EOLUS . . . . 29 years		EOCAID
OILLIOL . . . . 7 years		MOGFEIBE
ROS . . . . 7 years		EOCAID
ARDFEAR . . . . 18 years		GLAS
SEADNA I . . . . 10 years		EUNDA
SEADNA II . . . . 14 years		FEARARD
FIACA . . . . 9 years		CEAS
EOCAID **OLAM FODLA**		MARCAD
		NOID
		CEAS

The Table of Names of the Irish Provincial Kings

From 1000 BC to 700 BC

KINGS OF GAELEN OR LEINSTER

ERIMIONN . . . . 14 years	EOCAID (USURPER) 5 years
MUMNE . . . . 1 year	ERBOT
LAISNE . . . . 1 year	SMIOR GAAL
LUIGNE . . . . 1 year	FIACA
ERIAL . . . . 17 years	FIONN
ETERIAL . . . . 13 years	AONGUS
FILIAT . . . . 27 years	MAINE
TIGHERNMAS . . . . 27 years	ROITEASAC
	DON

NAMES OF IRISH DANAN CHIEFS MENTIONED

1. SEORL	2. CUIL	7. MAGN	8. THORL
3. FORB	4. MAGN I	9. DROMT	10. MAGN III
5. MEIRT	6. SCANDT I	11. MEIRT II	12. USGAR
		13. SCANDT II	

The Gaal of Sciot entered Eri a truly united people, but within two years of their arrival evil feeling came between the Chiefs of MUMAIN and GAELEN, resulting in a battle in which Iber was killed by the hand of his brother Iolar. After this the ARD-OLAM journeyed to the Northern Province, taking with him the 'Writings of Eolus', and the 'Chronicles of the Gael-ag', and did his part to educate the lad ER in the way of justice and truth.

Also as neither of the sons of Iber were of an age to rule, Iolar took upon himself the rule of the area of MUMAIN as well as GAELEN giving himself the title of 'ERIMION' – (meaning High King), this title was a cause of dispute for centuries, and the Southern Kingdoms had very little peace.

At the age of twenty five Er became of age to rule in ULLAD (ULSTER). He had been blessed with good teachers in the OLAM, while the corrupt Priesthood ('CRUIMTEAR') and their High Priest ('ARD-CRUIMTEAR') remained with the people of GAELEN and MUMAIN. According to the 'Chronicles' the influence of these CRUIMTEAR was too often the cause of trouble.

The rulers of ULLAD always curbed the power of the Cruimtear, and aimed for peace and friendship with the other provinces, and avoided being drawn into their disputes.

ER died after a rule of forty two years. He was interred at a place called Maginis – <u>where a heap was raised</u>. AOD, a Chief of the Land raised his voice, and said, **'Let this land be called for the times to come 'THE LAND OF ULLAD', a memorial of the First of the Race laid therein'**. In his footnotes, O'Connor says, **'ULLAD means a place of burial, from which the 'Kingdom of ULLAD', now ULSTER, had its name.'** (Volume Two pp 30).

It is also noted that MUMAIN (MUNSTER), was at first named DEAS, but from the death of Eocaid, MUMO, 'Chief of DEAS', the Province was re-named MUMAIN in respect of his name. (Volume Two pp 54).

About thirty years after the death of ER, when TIGHERNMAS was ruling in GAELEN, a ship came to the Coast with men from Feine (Spain) bringing letters, asking that his men might search and dig in the land for metals, offering a twentieth part-share of all that was found to be paid to the men of ERI, but the Sciot remembered the false dealings of the Feine in time past, and would have none of it. So the vessel returned as it came. Later another ship came with men bringing pillars, on which were similitudes of the Sun, Moon, and Stars, saying they had messages from BAAL, who wished to be remembered and worshipped by means of these. The Cruimtear willingly encouraged them, and persuaded Tighernmas to have the pillars set up. The Priests and Tighernmas bowed themselves down before the pillars, but the people made fun of them and said that they would not bow down before these pillars of stone. When the King saw how his action provoked his people against him, he put the blame on the Priests. Then the ARD-CRUIMTEAR taunted the King with being afraid of his people, and wished him to command the people to bow down before the Pillars. Tighernmas refused, and told the words of the Ard-Cruimtear to the congregation. On the morrow Tighernmas was found dead in his tent.

The Ard-Cruimtear told the people that Tighernmas had been struck by BAAL for his words spoken against the Cruimtear. The people did not believe him, but fell upon him, and slew him, together with all the Priests which they found, and threw down the pillars of stone which had been set up. Tighernmas ruled for twenty seven years.

From this time, the 'Chronicles' record the names and length of different Kings of MUMAIN and GAELEN, but deal mostly with events as they affect the Northern Kingdom and enter more fully into the History of ULLAD.

Rulers of Ireland as ARDI

From About 700 to 7 BC

EOCAID OLAM FODLA, ARDI 40 years	AOD (HUGH), ARDI 12 years
FIONN	"	20 years	ROS	"	1 year
EOCAID	"	17 years	CIOMBIOT	"	13 years
ARDFEAR	"	12 years	MACA (QUEEN) "	1 year
FIACA	"	8 years	REACTAD "	10 years
OILLIOL BEARN GAEL	"	12 years	UGOINE MOR . . . .
OILLIOL BEARNGNEAT	"	16 years	. . . ERIMIONN	"	30 years
SIORNA	"	20 years	GIALCAD	"	17 years
ROITEACTAC	"	7 years			
ELIM	"	1 year	DUAC	"	7 years
GIALCAD	"	9 years	DUAC	"	7 years
AIRT	"	12 years	MELGA	"	12 years
NUAD	"	13 years	MOGCORB	"	6 years
BREAS	"	9 years	AONGUS	"	7 years
EOCAID	"	1 year	CONGAL	"	7 years
FIONN	"	20 years	FEARCOB	"	7 years
SEADNA	"	15 years	CONLA	"	4 years
MURDAC	"	1 year	OILLIOL	"	25 years
DUAC	"	9 years	ADAMAIR	"	5 years
MUREDAC	"	5 years	EOCAID	"	7 years
EUNDA	"	5 years	FEARGUS	"	12 years
LUGAD	"	5 years	AONGUS TUIRMEAC 32 years
FIONN	"	16 years	CONAL	"	5 years
EOCAID	"	12 years	ADAMAIR	"	5 years
EOCAID	"	5 years	EUNDA AINE	"	10 years
LUGAD	"	4 years	CRIOMTAN	"	3 years
CONUIG	"	7 years	RUIDRUID MOR	7 years
AIRT	"	6 years	EUNDAMAIR	"	3 years
OILLIOL	"	9 years	BRESAIL	"	9 years
EOCAID	"	7 years	LUGAD	"	12 years
AIRGEADMAIR	"	30 years	CONGAL	"	6 years
DUAC	"	10 years	DUAC	"	7 years
LUGAD	"	4 years	FACTNA	"	23 years

Eocaid 'Olam Fodla' Ardi 700 BC

When the Sciot had been settled in ERI about three hundred years, EOCAID, the son of FIACA, of the race of ER, was chosen to rule in ULLAD. As a youth he was much loved by his people. He was brought up in all the wisdom of the OLAM, he delighted in horses and hunting.

Eocaid's first act was a battle with the 'PRINCE OF MUMAIN' who had spread an evil and false report concerning his father FIACA. The battle was fought on the soil of MUMAIN, and NOID, the King was slain. The anger of EOCAID was appeased and, with his warriors, he joined in the burial and mourning of NOID.

He and his warriors stayed in MUMAIN for nine days, and were charmed with the music of the harps, and tales of olden times, told by the Bards. EOCAID presented two beautiful horses and dogs to the brother of NOID, these animals in ULLAD seem to have much excelled those of MUMAIN and GAELEN. On his way back to ULLAD, Eocaid received and visited many of the Chiefs of the Land, renewing and strengthening the bond of friendship.

His journeying opened his eyes to the dis-union and discord prevailing between the Peoples of Eri, this led to his proposal to the Chiefs and Princes that they and the Chief representatives of the people should gather together every third year, with one chosen from among them – 'To sit one step higher than his fellows', and that all serious matters of dispute brought before them should be settled by the judgement of the many, instead of by battle and bloodshed, as had been hitherto. It would also be a time of feasting and means of strengthening friendship and knowledge of each other. The Chiefs agreed with EOCAID, and all decided to come together the following year, and to elect one who would be the 'Supreme Ruler' amongst them. The place chosen for the meeting was TOBRAD – now known as TARA which lies about ten miles North West of Dublin – (See Map), in the Province of the GAELEN. The meeting duly took place, and after listening to the wise reasoning of EOCAID, they unanimously chose him to be 'Supreme Ruler of ERI', under the title of 'ARDI'. He would not accept the Title of 'ERIMIONN', because the Title had caused so much dispute in the two Southern Kingdoms.

EOCAID – OLAM – FODLA ARDI is the Title by which he is distinguished in the 'Chronicles of Eri'. NEARTAN, the son of BEIRT, was ARD OLAM at that time, and was EOCAID'S trusted friend during the whole of his life. 'OLAM FODLA' (pronounced 'FEEOLAH') meaning 'Wonderful Prophet', and 'ARDI' meaning 'High King'.

Eocaid appointed Prince ROS, a Royal Chief of his own race **'to have an eye for the care of ULLAD'** – (Volume Two pp 93), while he dwelt in his tent in TOBRAD, to oversee the building of a Parliament House, which, when completed, was named 'TEACMOR', pp 95. O'Connor informs us that 'TOBRAD' means 'Hill of Election', pp 95. And TARA is a derivative of TORAH meaning 'Place of Divine Direction and Law'.

When the Parliament Building was completed, Eocaid sent out messengers for three of the Olam, and nine Heads of each of the Provinces, to come together, to make Laws for their Country. The letters saying, **'Let the Kings, Princes, and Nobles of the Gaal of Eri, and Chiefs of the Olam, and Heads of the People, meet at the High Chamber of Teacmor, on Tobrad, what time the fires shall be lighted on the summits of the plains of Eri'**, pp 96.

This custom of lighting Beacon Fires on the Summits became a continual practice at each triennial gathering. One can only imagine how wonderful that sight would be!

The Assembly came together. The Throne was set one step higher than the floor in the middle of the Chamber. A table stood on the floor beneath the throne. The King of MUMAIN took his seat at the table on the right side to the throne. The King of GAELEN took his seat opposite to the table, his face towards the throne.

And the King of ULLAD took his seat to the left hand side of the throne. All being accompanied by their Secretaries and Nobles. There were four Scribes, one for the Ardi, and one each for MUMAIN, GAELEN, and ULLAD. No man armed was allowed to stand on TOBRAD, neither would EOCAID allow the Cruimtear (Priests) to take any part in the Assembly or in the making of Laws. This enraged the Cruimtear, but the rule was not repealed then, or at any further time.

The Danaan sent their Nobles to the Assembly, expressing their desire that their Chief and Nobles might sit in the Assembly of Eri, in the High Chamber of Teacmor.

After some altercation and objection, especially from the King of GAELEN, who said, **'Shall the Danaan be admitted when the Ard-Cruimtear is denied?'**. But a vote was taken and goodwill prevailed, and it was arranged that the Danaan Chief, with eight of his Nobles should take their seats behind the throne, and take part in the proceedings.

In later years of Eocaid's rule, he was often much disturbed by the jealousies and ill-feeling of the Chief of GAELEN and MUMAIN against him. It seemed that they preferred the people to be kept in ignorance under the influence of the Cruimtear, rather than that they should acquire knowledge under the teachings of the OLAM, but the mass of the people loved and trusted Eocaid. THINGS HAVEN'T CHANGED IT SEEMS!!

This Assembly, unifying the various Provinces, was the first Central Government in Eri.

On the table, before the Throne, were the 'Rolls of Other Times', closed, and the 'Writings of Eolus', and 'The Chronicles of the Gaal', and 'Rolls' open to receive the words of the days as they pass, for the eye of the children of the land, that are yet to come. So a record was kept of all the proceedings, Laws were made, and all things in order. The concluding ceremony was the reading of the 'Words of Eolus', and the 'Chronicles', and if none were waiting for justice, the Assembly went forth, and the doors of the High Chamber were closed. Then the people enjoyed music, dancing, sports, and Tales of other Times until one moon had passed.

The Laws of Eri

The 'Laws of Eri' were codified and simplified by Eocaid when he met with the Assembly on TARA hill. It is significant that the first of the five Laws which the Kings of Eri adopted was the first one that was adopted by the family of NOAH immediately after the Deluge, **'Whoso sheddeth man's**

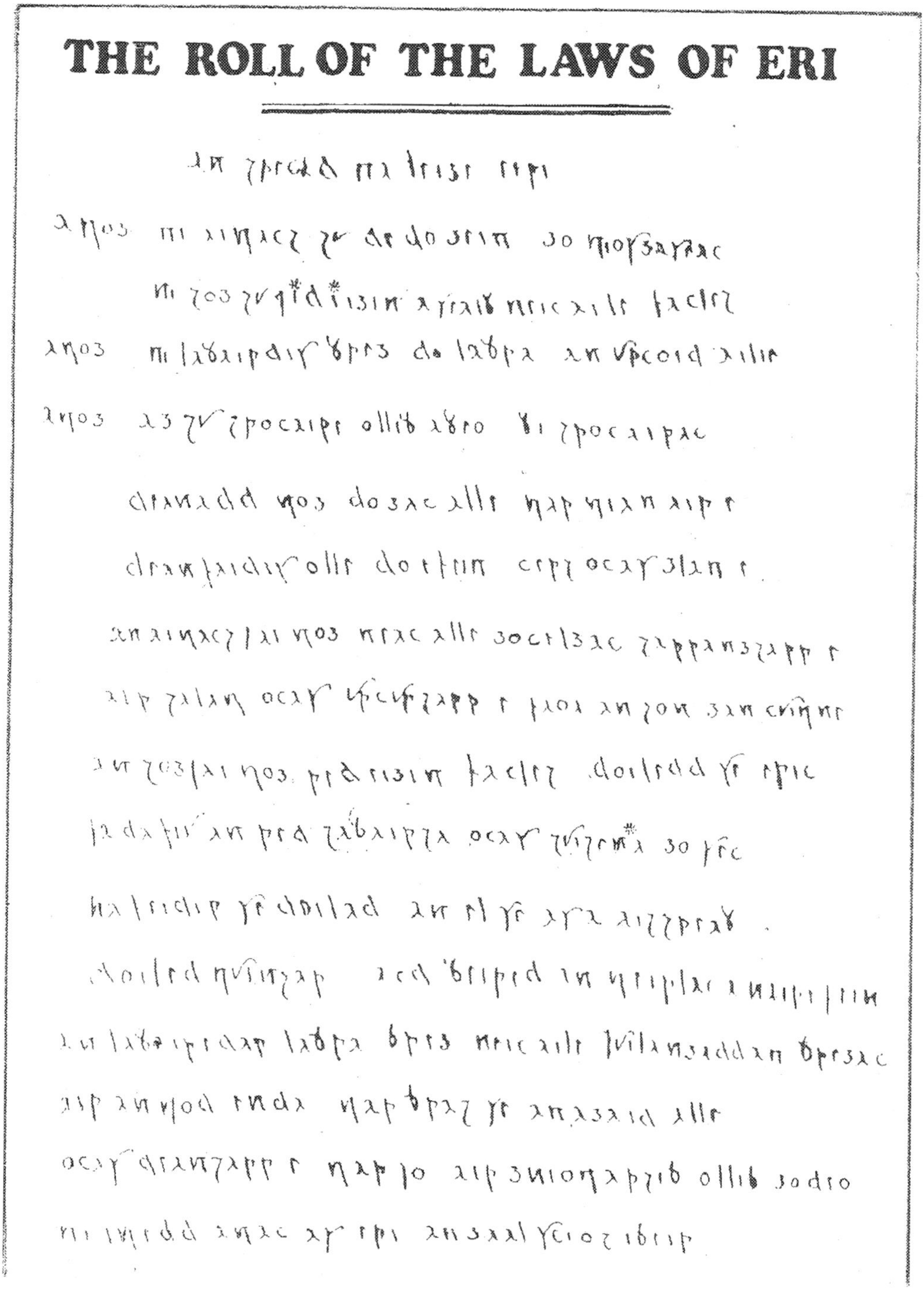

Fig. 13: Roll of the Laws of Eri

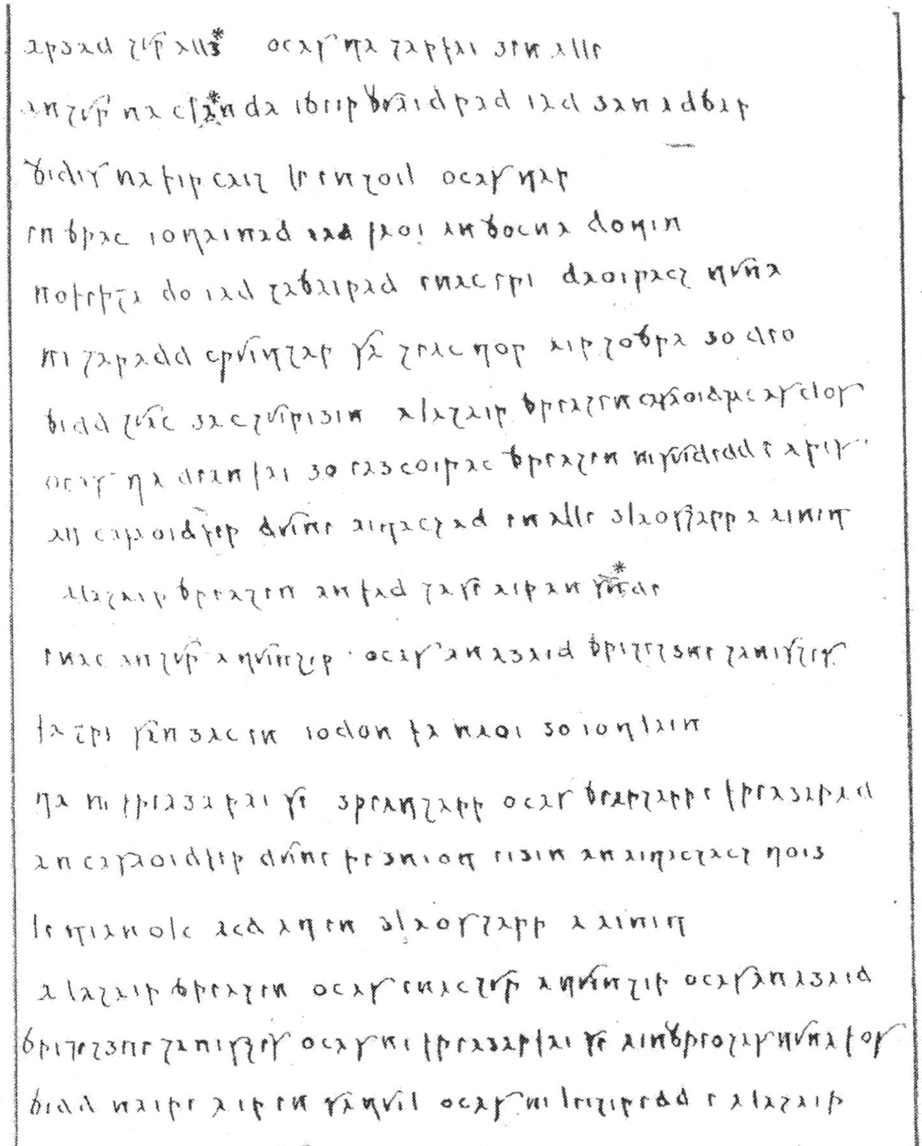

Fig. 14: Roll of the Laws of Eri

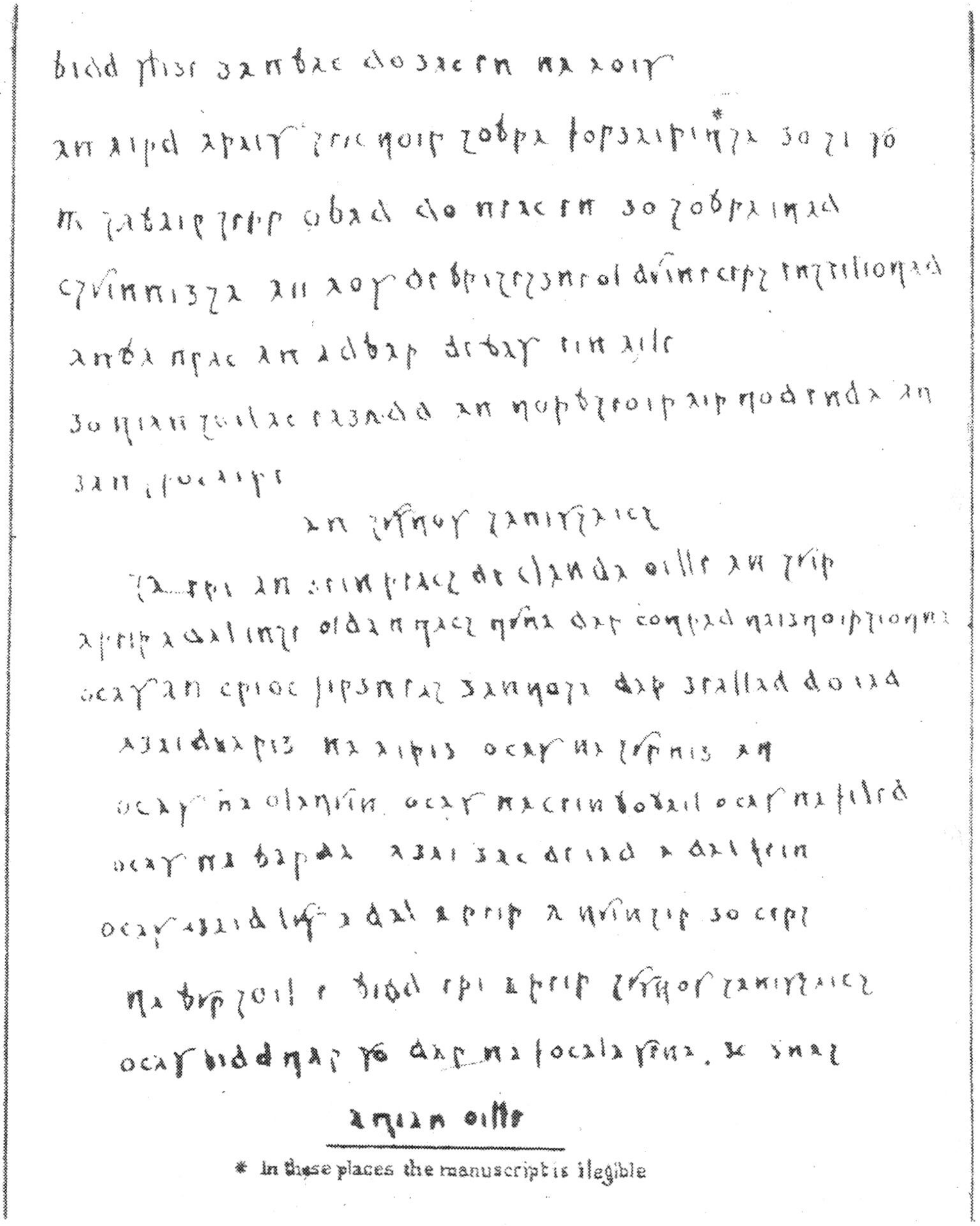

Fig. 15: Roll of the Laws of Eri

The Interior of the High Chamber of Teacmor on Tobrad

(During the Convention of the National Assembly of Eri)

Fig. 16: The Interior of the High Chamber of Teacmor on Tobrad

(During the conventions of the national assemblies of Eri)

Eocaid remained at TOBRAD, and was intent on building a house nearby for the OLAM, where the youths of the land might be instructed, but the rains and cold weather prevented the work.

Many years before the reign of Eocaid, SOBAIRCE, King of ULLAD had built a palace, near to the present day town of CARRICKFERGUS, which he named DUN-SOBAIRCE, and which the palace was known by thereafter. All the Kings of Ulster resided there, during their reign. (Volume 2 pp 37-38)

In his notes on page eleven, O'Connor also informs us that, **'At this day the haven of the river BOYNE is called IMBAR-COLBA, from the Prince COLBA'**, who was drowned with CIER.

Eocaid journeyed back to his home in ULLAD, **'As he passed through the Land of Geinter (Fermanagh), he did chance to see TATLA, a damsel of that land, she was fair, very fair, and lived with her widowed Mother, and Eocaid took her unto him as his wife.'**

This marriage united the people of ULSTER and FERGNEAT into one united province, even as it is to this day.

It will have been noted that the FERGNEAT were not given a place in the Assembly of the Tara Kings in Teacmor on Tobrad, and the reason is not given in 'The Chronicles', but by this marriage they were represented by the King of ULSTER.

Eocaid went on to DUN-SOBAIRCE, where a Great Assembly of his own people met him, and there was mirth and great joy for nine days. After this Eocaid appointed FEARGUS, a Prince, to be King in ULLAD in his stead, and, with one of the OLAM and MORDA, Chief Judge, to represent ULLAD at Teacmor. And especially did he charge FEARGUS to see to the building of Colleges in which the OLAM could teach the youth of the land in all wisdom and learning, these Colleges were called, MUR-OLAMIN. In after times Eocaid delighted to visit them and encourage all in the search for knowledge. 'The Chronicles' say, **'Every tongue in ULLAD is loud in FEARGUS'S praise. He ruleth the land in truth, wisdom and mercy.'**

We are informed that one of the prime duties of the OLAM was to build Fire Beacons across the Summits of ERI every three years, to signal the holding of the Parliament on Tara Hill. Eri received the name of <u>BREO-LAN</u>, to distinguish it from <u>BREO-TAN</u> (Britain), and <u>BREO-CCEAN</u> (Gael-ag in Spain). The other duties were to maintain Fire Beacons on all the promontories around the coasts for the guidance of shipping. The islands like those of Britain and Gael-ag must have presented a fantastic sight to the seafarers.

At one triennial assembly on Tobrad, a message came from Feargus in Dun-Sobairce to Eocaid, **'Tatla doth lay on the bed of sickness, her eye doth long to look on her beloved.'** Eocaid took his departure for Dun-Sobairce, and in six days she was no more. Tatla was returned to Geinter and interred there.

Traditions

The traditions and songs of the bards which have been passed down, speak of the arrival in Eri of a great sage from the East, with his Scribe, and an Hebrew Princess and her retinue.

That sage was JEREMIAH, his attendant, BARUCH the Scribe, and the Princess, one of the 'King's Daughters', that is, daughter of King Zedekiah, the last reigning King of the Tribe of Judah, of the Dynasty of David.

Dr. O'Connor's chronological reckoning fixes the beginning of the Rule of Eocaid Olam Fodla 700 BC, which is nearly one hundred years before the time of Jeremiah, who prophecied 629 – 590 BC. Seeing, however, that the earliest history of the Gaal-Sciot-Iber had been passed down orally from Father to son, until the wise ruler Eolus learned to write, and collected and commenced keeping the 'Chronicles of His Race', it does seem possible that there would be a miscalculation of years or more probable still, would be the difference in the reckoning of calendars of the Jews and those of the Gaal Sciot. In our frontispiece 'Ring of Baal' – that is, the calendar of the Sciot, we are shown thirteen periods making 'one ring' (year). By this it seems that the Sciot had 'thirteen months' of four weeks each, a period of three hundred and sixty four days (fifty two weeks), but we are not given any further information.

So it is possible that there was a difference in calendar reckoning, and that the year in which Jeremiah brought the Princess <u>Tephi</u> to Ireland, corresponded with the reign of Eocaid, and that she was the <u>Tatla</u> whom Eocaid married.

Geinter was very accessible from the Western Sea by the mouth of the River Erne, which was the river that flowed through Geinter. Tatla was greatly beloved by Eocaid. She died young leaving two sons, FIONN, EOCAID, and a daughter, FIONA, who became the wife of the King of MUMAIN.

Eocaid sorrowed greatly. He returned to Dun-Sobairce, saying unto Neartan, the Ard Olam, **'Every step I take, everything I look upon here, reminds me of TATLA'.** No other such woman in all the 'Chronicles of Eri' is written of with such honour and admiration.

It is she whom the Bards and tradition have glorified so greatly under the name of <u>TEPHI</u>. <u>If so, her tomb will not be found near TARA, but at OMAGH, not far from FERMANAGH</u>, which was in ancient times, an important site, and which in the days of Eocaid was known as AOIMAG, and a Chief of AOIMAG is mentioned occasionally.

AOIMAG was the name by which the Gaal of Sciot of Iber knew the land of Palestine. The fact that the same name was given to a tract in ULLAD favours the idea that there were settlers from AOIMAG who remembered it with affection. If therefore, Tatla was Tephi, the daughter of Zedekiah, who was Jeremiah? It could only be Feargus! If Feargus was Jeremiah, he certainly realized in Eri the promise that he should build and plant (JER. 1: 10), for Eocaid caused him to rule over ULLAD, and especially gave him charge of MUR-OLAMAIN at DUN-SOBAIRCE, which was to be the first 'SCHOOL OF THE OLAM' (Prophets) in Eri!

If in Feargus we see Jeremiah, in the Ard Olam NEARTAN we can discern the Scribe BARUCH, the son of NERIAH, NEARTAN being so close to NERIAH. It is possible that he too would appear under a different name. These are just conjectures. However, the Ancestry of the Ancient Scottish and Irish Kings trace back to this period, and through which our present Queen Elizabeth II had descended, tracing her line back through these Kings to the Royal House of David and Solomon, Kings of Israel!

Some time after the death of Tatla, Eocaid took AMARIL, the <u>daughter of Prince Ross of ULSTER</u>, as his Queen, she gave him two sons ARDFEAR and CAIRBRE.

FIONN son

EOCAID son } by Tatla

FIONA daughter

ARDFEAR son } by Amaril

CAIRBRE son

Eocaid ruled Ulster for forty years, and ruled over all Ireland as ARDI for a further twenty eight years. He was laid to rest beneath 'his Heap'. The whole congregation stood around the heap, and NEARTAN, from its summit, concluded with the words, **'His spirit will be immortal'**, and the congregation took their departures. According to the 'Chronicles' this would be the year 663 BC.

Medallion Portrait of Jeremiah in
the historic Four Courts in Dublin.

Fig. 17: Medallion Portrait of Jeremiah in the
Historic Four Courts in Dublin

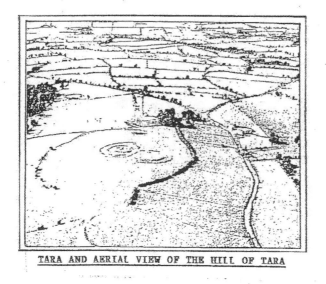

TARA AND AERIAL VIEW OF THE HILL OF TARA

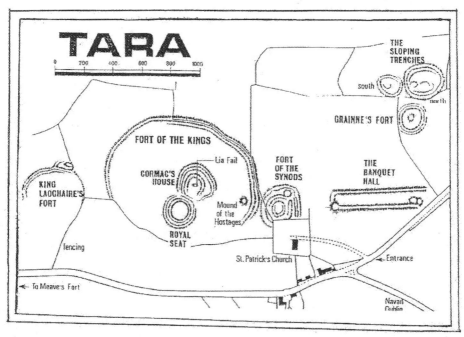

Fig. 18: Tara – An Aerial View of the Hill of Tara

New Evidence for the Westward Move of King Zedekiah's Daughters and the Coronation Stone From Palestine to the Isles of the West

There is at Laughcrew, Co. Meath, Southern Ireland, an ancient stone seat with incised markings which was examined by Sir James Fergusson of the Royal Irish Academy in 1872, who stated that it is without doubt a royal seat or throne, and was probably the official seat of the great Irish King and law-maker, Ollamph Fodhia (Ollam Fola).

At first sight the markings look like childish scribbling; Bronze Age doodling, but on a closer examination the surprising possibility is that they may be a very crudely drawn map of the move of 'the King's daughters and Jeremiah the prophet and Jacob's Stone of Bethal, Lia Fail, from Palestine to Ireland.

Although no recognizable outline of the Mediterranean is used, the main locations in the story all appear in approximately the right places, although grossly distorted and out of scale. If indeed this is a map the cartographer knew approximately where geographical locations lay.

To the right of the picture, the East, appears large and clear an enclosed area where Jerusalem lies. Beneath it, a hooked arrow line pointing in the direction of the royal party's move: south to Egypt.

To the left of the arrow is another large enclosure where the fortress of Tahpanhes would be, with three lines below it possibly indicating the various tracks and routes into Egypt which passed the fortress.

Above 'Tahpanhes' is a crude representation of a ship, with passengers, and to the south west of Tahpanhes, in the correct geographical location, is Egypt and the River Nile.

To the north of 'Jeremiah's ship' is a scattered group of small circles where the various small Greek islands would be, further West appears to be marked a deviation to Spain, where, according to the Irish Annales, Scota, Zedekiah's daughter, had her second son, Heremon, by her husband Gathelus.

At the top centre is the sun and moon, indicating a long journey over several days and nights, and to the south west that which might be the Pleiades constellation, a useful marker for the navigator.

To the far west is a large spiral enclosure, indicating the position of the then mainly inhabited area of Ireland, even including beneath it a small circle where the present day Saltee Island would be. In its correct position to the north is an oval enclosure where Tara would be, the dotted line possibly indicating a fenced off, fortified enclosure, and connecting the East with the West: Palestine with Ireland, a long, snake-like line through the Mediterranean, the multitudinous curves indicating much tacking against the prevailing westerly winds.

Perhaps the most surprising feature of all, in the top left hand corner, is the rough outline of a bird, possibly an eagle (which has lost its left foot) and seemingly carrying a twig in its beak, which puts us in mind of Ezekiel's veiled hint of 'the tender twig', Israel's royal princess, being set down in a far distant land where the royal throne would be carried on.

Extremely crude though this drawing is, each of the main factors or locations in this romantic story appear in approximately their right places, even to a series of 'ponds' or 'lakes' in the extreme south east where today the bitter Lakes and Lake Timsah are located in the Suez Canal Zone.

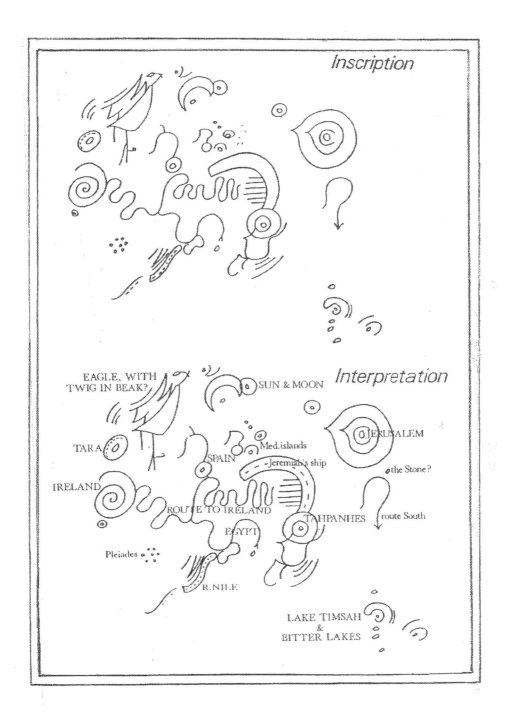

Fig. 19: Interpretation of the Laughcrew Inscription

Tea-Tephi or Scota

There are currently two opinions in circulation about the name of the king's daughter, through whom the Royal Descent from David was transferred from Palestine to Britain: was she Tea-Tephi or Scota?

Ever since the publication in 1840 of John Wilson's book *Our Israelitish Origin*, it has been realised that the Royal House of Britain must have been descended from the Biblical House of David to whom God made promises of an enduring dynasty. Since our own royal house can, without difficulty, trace its ancestry back to the ancient kings of Ireland, it was necessary to find a connecting link with the last kings of Judah. The Bible tells us that all the sons of Zedekiah were slain, but that the king's daughters were taken to Egypt with Jeremiah, after which no more was heard from them (Jer. 43: 5-7).

According to traditional Irish history, Ireland was ruled by a Milesian dynasty for at least a thousand years before the birth of Christ, and before that by sundry 'Pre-Milesian' peoples, the last of whom were the Tuatha De Danaan. The Rev. F. R. A. Glover, without proper evidence, jumped to the conclusion that one of the king's daughters made her way to Ireland along with Jeremiah, and there married the reigning monarch. In seeking evidence to support his theory in Irish history, he picked on a lady named Tea who married Heremon, the first Milesian king of Ireland, and he made out that she was also called Tephi.

Glover published this theory in 1861, and a second edition of his book, *England, the Remnant of Judah*, appeared in 1881 shortly before he died. His ideas were then adopted by an American professor of Military Tactics, C. A. L. Totten, in the first five volumes of *Our Race*, published in 1890-92. He was followed by Rev. W. M. H. Milner in *The Royal House of Britain, an Enduring Dynasty* in 1902, of which the enlarged edition of 1908 has since been repeated many times.

About 1953 an alternative view was put forward by C. F. Parker, and was published in the Bible Research Handbook, serials 113-118. He pointed out that according to Irish history Miletus, father of Heremon, and founder of the Milesian dynasty, had married a lady known as Scota in Egypt before he migrated to Spain on the way to Ireland. At least this theory has the merit of locating the lady in Egypt, a feature that is entirely lacking in the case of Tea-Tephi.

Glover's Sources

Without any proper evidence that Tea had come from Egypt, Glover claimed to find this in some old Irish tracts on the origin of the name Temor for Tara, the ancient seat of the Irish kings. Three such documents had been published by George Petrie in 1839, and again by O'Conellan in 1846 in the notes to his translation of *The Annals of Ireland (1171-1616)*. Glover refers to both these sources, but quoted only those parts that suited his purpose, ignoring the first one altogether.

The first of these tracts was composed by Amergin, chief bard of Dermod, monarch of Ireland in the sixth century. It is summarised by O'Conellan thus:

> '*Teph or Tephi, a daughter of Bachtir, king of Spain, having been married to Chanthon, king of Britain, died there, but her body was brought back to Spain, and a* mur *or mound was erected to her memory, and called* Tephi-mur, *or the Mound of Tephi. Tea, daughter of Lugaidh, son of Ith, and queen of Heremon, the first Milesian monarch of Ireland, having seen the mound of Tephi while in Spain, she caused a similar mound to be constructed when she came to Ireland, as a sepulchral monument for herself; and being buried there, it was called* Tea-mur, *signifying Tea's mound, and hence was derived the name of Tara. (p. 294)'*

The full text of this tract in Gaelic, with an English translation, is given in Petrie's paper on Tara, pages 129-131 of the *Transactions of the Royal Irish Academy*, Vol. 18 (1839).

The second document produced by Petrie and O'Connellan is a poem attributed to Fintan, a bard of the sixth century. This makes no mention at all of Tephi, but it agrees with the first document in saying that Tea was the wife of Heremon, and the daughter of Lugaidh, and that Teamhair was named after her.

The third document is a poem attributed to Cuan O'Lochain who died in 1024, but Petrie points out that the language shows it to be some centuries older than that. It comprises eighteen stanzas, or 72 lines, of which Glover appears to publish 42, but actually only 38, since he quotes verse 8 a second time with a different translation of the first line. The first four stanzas relate that Heremon provided a mound for Tea when she died. Verses 5-15 then give an account of the marriage of Tephi, daughter of Cino Bachtir, to Canthon, a British king, and the return of her body to Spain when she died, and the building of her sepulchre there. Verse 16 explains that this was the model from which Temor, or Tara, was copied. It reads:-

'It was in that place, according to arrangement

They nobly constructed the first model

For that of Temor, of unrivalled form

And of delightful and elegant aspect.'

Petrie gives a similar translation, and in a footnote (p. 135) says, 'The meaning is, that the tomb which was erected in Spain for Tephi was the model after which Heremon built the monument or *mur* of Tea on the hill of Temur, from which it took its name.'

Immediately following the poem O'Connellan gives the following summary:-

'It appears from the foregoing poem that Tephi, therein mentioned, daughter of Cino Bactir, king of Brigantia in Spain, was married to Canthon, king of Britain, and as a guarantee that her body should be restored for burial in Spain, the chief idol of the Britons, called Etherun or Taran, was left as a pledge with the king of Spain; and Canthon, king of Britain, having restored the body of Tephi, she was

buried in a sepulchral mound, from which was derived the name of Temor or Tara.'

It is evident from these old sources that Tea and Tephi were two different women. Tephi, the daughter of the leader of the Celtic settlement in Spain, had been married to Canthon, a British king. She is otherwise unkown to Irish history. Tea, on the other hand, is a well known person in Irish histories, where she is always said to be the daughter of Lugaidh, the son of Ith, the son of Breogan. She married Heremon, son of Miletus, in Spain before the sons of Miletus migrated to Ireland. Since her ancestry is well known, she cannot have been a daughter of any king of Judah.

The Story of Scota

In an article *Who were the Scots?*, published in *The National Message*, June 1970, W. E. Filmer pointed out that there were at least two separate groups of Israelites migrating along the Mediterranean Sea from Asia Minor to Spain. The first group to arrive founded a city called Brigantium in the northwest, after passing through the Straits of Gibraltar. The leader of this group is given the eponymous name Breogan in the Irish histories; he was the great-grandfather of Tea.

Another group of Israelites travelled by way of Egypt. Their leader Gaythelus, or Miletus, went to Egypt and assisted Pharaoh Psammitichus in his war against the Ethiopians, and received in reward Scota, said to be the daughter of Pharaoh, to wife, after which they migrated to Spain. Scota was probably one of the king's daughters whom Jeremiah had taken to Egypt. Since the king's name is not mentioned, she could have been the daughter of either Josiah or Zedekiah.

Miletus had six sons by Scota, one of whom was Heremon who married Tea in Spain. It is suggested that Miletus had been among the Cimmerian group of Israelites ravaging Asia Minor at that time. Since these Cimmerians included captives taken by Sennacherib in 701 BC, some of them would be of the tribe of Judah, for Sennacherib came 'up against all the fenced cities of Judah and took them' (2 Kings 18: 13). It is possible, therefore, that Miletus could have been a Judahite. This is important, since inheritance through the female line could take place only if the lady married one of her own tribe.

The following table illustrates the suggested relationship between the two ladies Scota and Tea:-

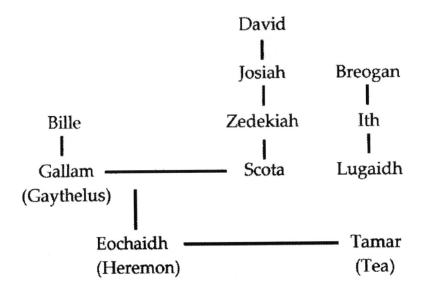

* See complete pedigree on pages 218-9 of this book.

* This history is dealt with in greater 'scriptural' detail in Chapter (11) Eleven, pages 169-196 of my book: IN THE ISLES OF THE SEA.   ISBN 1-4120-7417-7. TRAFFORD PUBLISHING Co. – now a division of AUTHOR SOLUTIONS, 1663 LIBERTY DRIVE, BLOOMINGTON, INDIANA, 47403, USA. Tel. 001-888-232-4444.

Chapter Ten

The Scottish Connection

Fionn had succeeded Feargus, as King in ULLAD, when he became of age, and now upon the death of Eocaid he was elected as ARDI. During the reign of his Father, the Reigning Monarchs of the Mumain, Gaelen and Danaan had been the cause of much trouble causing disputes and fighting. Eocaid had taken several hostages from among the families of the other kings. These hostages lived with him at his palace in Dun-Sobairce, by this method he was able to exercise firm control over the Kings of Eri. Fionn continued with the same practice during his rule as ARDI.

Neartan, the ARD-OLAM who had served Eocaid faithfully was now of very old age, and requested that Fionn would release him from his duties.

> *'And Fionn said, 'Let Neartan do what is pleasing unto himself; should Fionn require his counsel, Neartan will not withhold it.'*
>
> *And Fionn did embrace Neartan, calling him the friend of Eocaid.*
>
> *And Ross was chosen ARD-OLAM of ULLAD, in the place of Neartan, the son of Beirt.'*

(Volume 2 pp 204)

'The Chronicles of Eri' had been faithfully kept by the ARD-OLAM since the days of King Eolus, who had reigned over the Gaal Sciot Iber in Spain, circa

1475 BC. Why was Prince Ross of the Royal Family made ARD-OLAM of all Eri? It was a diplomatic ploy!

With the appointment of Ross as ARD-OLAM, FIONN forever broke the power of the Cruimtear (Priests), and their ARD-CRUIMTEAR, which, many times in the past, and more recently during the reign of his Father, had threatened the sovereignty and peace of Ireland. As I said, things haven't changed in Ireland!

The year 663 BC was a great day in Irish History. Fionn started his reign as ARDI, following in his Father's footsteps, and reigned twenty years as ARDI, and during this period the ARD-OLAM of all Ireland was his own blood relative, Prince Ross, who had served a period as 'Caretaker Ruler' of ULLAD, appointed to this position by Eocaid whilst he was busy building Teacmor on Tobrad (Volume 2 pp 93).

This was a smart move on the part of FIONN. Prince Ross would be allowed to accompany him to the Triennial Meetings of the Eri Parliament at Teacmor on Tobrad, whereas the Priests (Cruimtear) had been disallowed from ever attending the Assembly of the High Chamber.

The result of this action by FIONN had far greater connotations to it than first seemed, for by it Ross and his descendants, 'The Clan Ross' were now committed to the office of ARD-OLAM, and 'Priesthood' of that office for the next 2,000 years, though they were primarily of Royal blood.

This commitment of the Clan Ross was to flower in later years, in forming the Celtic Church in Scotland, when in 557 AD, Columba transplanted Christianity from Ireland to the Isle of Iona.

Descendants of Ross were given the great promontory of ROSS-SHIRE in Scotland (Sciot-land), by Columba, as the base for establishing Christianity in that land. Thus, the character of the future Church of Scotland (Sciot-land) was formed 1,100 years before the adventure into Dalriada, headed by Columba. In that new religion with their 'KIRKS' ('CHI-UR-CHI') having no Bishops, but Presbyters, to provide the Spiritual Leadership for the SCIOTS.

The Clan Ross, as Royalty, were given possession of the land known as Ross-shire, and as Christian Missionaries, they founded their first Mission at 'Applecross', on the Western Shores of Ross. Here, they were known as 'HAGGARTS', which is the Gaelic word for 'Priests'.

The Ross promontory was steadily settled by the Clan Ross, who as zealous Christians, sought to found a new SCIOT-LAND in the North.

To their minds it was the beginning of the Kingdom of God on Earth. However, in forming a Church they in fact, formed a Nation.

Hume Brown, the Historian, wrote, **'Scottish History may be emphatically said to begin with Columba's landing in Iona, about the year AD 563. By the great work he achieved Columba fairly takes his place with the founders of Nations, who have a niche apart in the annals of mankind.'**

The most celebrated of Columba's disciples was BAITHENE, Columba's successor at the Abbey of Iona. CORMAC, the Navigator, was the first Missionary to the Lewis and the Orkneys, North and South Uist and Barra. MACHAR was sent to establish a 'KIRK' at Aberdeen. DROSTON was the founder of the Monastery at Deer. Beginning at Iona, these zealous Missionaries erected huge carved Celtic Stone Crosses to mark their progress as they moved Northwards. At Tain in 'Easter Ross' stood the shrine of the Celtic Saint DUTHAC, which became a Sanctuary to which JAMES IV made annual pilgrimages in the 15th Century.

It has been indicated that the Royalty of Northern Ireland extends back to 1700 - 1600 BC, with the migration into Ireland of the CALCOL/ZARAH branch of the 'HOUSE OF JUDAH'. The descendants of the 'Scarlet Thread'.

In the 'Arms of Northern Ireland', we find centred, on a Red Cross, a White Star of David, within which is seen a Red Hand, above which is the 'Crown of Royalty'.

There is also another emblem in Northern Ireland, a White Shield, upon which we see the Red Hand and Cord of Zarah/Judah!

Another distinguishing mark of Zarah/Judah, is their exclusive use of the Rampant Red Lion in their Heraldry, in contrast to the Tawny Couchant Lion of Pharez/Judah. The Zarahites were already settled in Northern Ireland some 400 years before the arrival of the Tuatha-de-Danaan (Tribe of Dan), about 1200 BC.

Having the same heritage, and the same language, they lived together in comparative harmony, with the descendants of Zarah/Judah and Er, in Northern Ireland, gaining ascendancy, having their divine right as part of 'The Royal Family of Judah'.

The name of Ross can be closely identified with the Red Hand and Cord of Zarah/Judah.

The 'S' in Gaelic is pronounced as 'Z', so that Ross is pronounced Roz or Rose. The Red Hand of Zarah can be any shade of Red, from pink to deep red, as used in Heraldry.

The Red Hand represents the hand of the twin son Zarah, which showed first, before his brother Pharez, which the midwife took, and tied a thread around it to distinguish him as the first born of Judah. Eventually, as we have shown previously, Pharez was declared heir, and it was from him that the official branch of the 'Tribe of Judah' and the 'Davidic Royal House' is descended. However, with the marriage of TATLA or TEPHI? of the Pharez branch to Eocaid, a Royal Prince of the Zarah branch, the 'breach' was healed (Genesis 38).

Fig. 20: Colour Chart: The County Shields of Ireland – Showing

The Red Hand Symbol of Zarah-Judah

Land of the Flaming Fires in the Isles of the Sea

The descendants of Ross in Scotland were called 'O'BREO-LAN', meaning from the 'Land of the Flaming Fires', or 'Eri-land'.

Quoting from the 'Chronicles of Eri', **'the office of the Olam is to guard the fires, to guide the foot of the wayfaring ones in the darkness of the night, and to note the seasons.'**

The prime job of the Olam was to build fires on the summits of Eri, to signal the holding of Parliament on Tobrad (Tara), and on all the promontories and headlands to guide the seafarer.

The assignment of Prince Ross, as ARD-OLAM placed him in charge of all the OLAM who's duty it was to build and keep the fires.

Therefore, the name O'BREO-LAN was not a family name for those descendants of Ross who settled in Scotland, but the name indicated Ireland, which was widely known as 'The Land of the Flaming Fires'.

As heretofore mentioned, this same custom was observed on the coasts of Cornwall and Devon when the Sciot assisted the Phoenician Mine Owners in their Mining Operation there. This habit spread around the Coast of Southern Britain, North as far as Cumbria, Westmoreland, Northumbria, Lancashire, and Yorkshire. The island was called BREO-TAN. The Yorkshire Celts being known as BREO-CCEAN-TIES which was eventually corrupted to BRIGANTES by the Romans!

We can now read ISAIAH 24: 15-16:-

> *'Wherefore glory ye the Lord in the fires, even the name of the Lord God of Israel, in the isles of the sea.*
>
> *From the uttermost <u>part</u> of the earth have we heard songs, even glory to the righteous...'*

Isn't this amazing! '<u>PART</u>' here in this Scripture is singular, meaning some specific island<u>s</u> which is plural, meaning a cluster of islands at the uttermost part of the earth.

Again see <u>ISAIAH 42: 10, 12</u>:-

> *'Sing unto the Lord a new song, and his praise from the <u>end</u> of the earth, ye that go down to the sea, and all that is therein; the isles and the inhabitants thereof.*
>
> *Let them give glory unto the Lord, and declare his praise in the islands.'*

In this Scripture the word is 'END' i.e. 'END OF THE EARTH'; singular, not ENDS plural.

To the ancients, even in the days of Isaiah, the **'uttermost part'**, or **'End of the earth'**, was the continent of Europe, for many years, only the Phoenician Sea Merchants knew of the Islands of Britain and Ireland, they guarded their secret closely, even to the point of wrecking or scuttling their ships if they were being followed, to guard the secret of their source of metals.

In fact the Romans named the furthest point West '<u>FINNIS-TERRA</u>'. 'The Finish of the Land', now known as Cape FINNISTERRE in Spain.

It was not until the late years BC that they were informed of the islands of the sea.

Now let us read ISAIAH 49: 12:-

> *'Behold, these shall come from far: and lo, these from the north and from the west...'*

In this statement Isaiah identifies the geographical location of the islands in the sea, at the uttermost **'Part'** or End of the earth.

He specifies them as being North West of Palestine! In the Ancient Hebrew there was no such expression as North West, so Isaiah renders it North and West.

The only islands residing in the sea at the uttermost **'Part'** and **'End'** of the Continent of Europe are the British Isles! No other islands fit the description.

The whole of Isaiah's message from Chapter Forty to Chapter Sixty Six is for the people of God, descendants of Shem – Eber (Iber) – Abraham – Isaac and Jacob residing in the Isles of the Sea.

Remember that the Island of Britain and Ireland began to be inhabited by these Hebrew settlers nearly <u>1,000 years BEFORE Isaiah was born</u>!

Isaiah does not explain the message contained in what he calls his **'burdens'** – why? – because he expected his listeners and readers to know those to whom he was addressing, even those who would read his **'burdens' in future years – especially those Hebrews in the Isles of the Sea! Yes! Even you! And if you cannot accept this one essential fact, then you will never ever understand the writings of Isaiah – it will forever remain a mystery.**

Furthermore Isaiah declares:-

> *'For with stammering lips and another tongue will the Lord speak to his people.'*

(Isaiah 28: 11)

Strongs Concordance gives the Hebrew word for stammering as 'GAEL' while Youngs Analytical Concordance gives stammering as 'LEAG'. It is most striking therefore that one of the old names for the Irish Scots should be 'LEAGAEL', or in Hebrew, a stammering people, the double word representing the left to right Phoenician, and the right to left Hebrew!

The Scottish Declaration of Independence – 6th April 1320 AD

This document is sometimes referred to as the 'Declaration of Arbroath'.

Much of the material found in the 'Chronicles of Eri' are borne out by this Ancient Document, issued by King Robert Bruce, <u>6th April 1320 AD</u>.

This document is of supreme interest, but which is seen by few, and further still, it is unknown to many, owing to their ignorance of its existence, lying in the Register-House at Edinburgh, Scotland. This document is a parchment to which are attached some twenty red and green seals (being the seals of subscribing Scottish Nobles).

It was drawn up by Bernard-de-Linton, 'Abbot of Aberbrothock' and 'Chancellor of Scotland in the year 1320, and was sent to Pope John XXII by the Scottish Estates in Parliament assembled in the 'Abbey of Aberbrothock' under the Presidency of King Robert the Bruce, 6th April, 1320 AD. Officials of the Register-House have described it as, **'probably our most precious possession'**, and it may be seen in a shallow glass case in the Register-House at Edinburgh.

King Edward I of England had failed in his attempt to subjugate Scotland, having met a crushing defeat at the 'Battle of Bannockburn' in 1317 AD. He enlisted support of the Pope (John XXII) to whom he sent lavish gifts of jewels, as a result of which the Pope refused to acknowledge the Bruce as King of Scotland, and indeed sent emissaries to him with a view to securing his submission to the English King. These papal messengers, Cardinal Gaucelin and Cardinal Luke, were not received by the Scottish King, who would not even read their letters. Instead he summoned the Scottish Parliament, and the document proclaiming 'The Independence of the Scottish People' was drawn up and despatched.

The point of particular interest to us is the remarkable testimony which the document contains concerning the origin and previous migrations of the Scottish people, a declaration which, it must be remembered, is attested by the seals of not only King Robert the Bruce, but of all the Scottish Nobles of the day. It is not, therefore, a statement by a single (possibly fallible) historian, but the official declaration of a King and his Estates in Parliament assembled and consequently being of overwhelming authority.

> *'We know, Most Holy Father and Lord, and from the chronicles and books of the ancients gather, that among other illustrious nations, ours, to wit the nation of the Scots, has been distinguished by many honours; <u>which passing from the greater Scythia through the Mediterranean Sea and Pillars of Hercules</u>, and sojourning in Spain among the most savage tribes through a long course of time, could nowhere be subjugated by any people however barbarous; <u>and coming thence one thousand two hundred years after the outgoing of the people of Israel</u>, they, by many victories and infinite toil, acquired for themselves the possessions in the West which they now hold .... In their kingdom one hundred and thirteen kings of their own royal stock, no stranger intervening, have reigned.'*

It is surely deeply interesting to have this statement, so unimpeachably attested, <u>that the ancestors of the Scottish people came from Greater Scythia</u>, sojourned a while in Spain <u>and settled in Scotland 1,200 years after the going out of the people of Israel</u>.

Further information can be obtained from Volume I of the Acts of Parliament of Scotland, or Part II of the National Manuscripts of Scotland, or from the 'Scot's Magazine' issue April 1934, from which the illustration is produced.

Of course there are these so called 'historians' who surmise that the 'Declaration' was based on the long procedure of a Master Baldred Bisset of 1301 AD; and that Baldred's account of the origin of the Scots (from Greater Scythia to Spain, Ireland, and to Scotland) was altered to make more palatable, the claim of Robert Bruce to be the legitimate heir to the throne of a sovereign Scotland, and to...

> *'make the conversion of the Scots to Christianity by the Apostle Andrew, brother of Peter, sound more plausible. For one of the very few reasonably early statements recorded about Saint Andrew was that he had preached to the Scythians. There was a stubborn tradition that the Picts had come from Scythia, and the letter of 1320 seems to be an early example of the confusion of Pictish and Scottish origins.'*

(G. W. S. Barrow: 'Robert the Bruce' pp 426)

Now we ask you, would Robert the Bruce and the Scottish Nobles mentioned in the 'Declaration' knowingly put their 'Seals' to a statement or document that they knew to be false? Would these Earls, Barons, Freeholders, and 'The whole Community of the Realm of Scotland', subscribe to a fraud enacted in the Scottish Parliament? Of course not. These were men of honour and dignity, they would not have placed their 'Seals' to a falsehood, and to imply so commits a terrible injustice to their character and nobility.

The King and his Noblemen declared their independence from any other Nation, declaring that ... **'They journeyed from Greater Scythia by way of the Tyrrhenian Sea (Mediterranean) and the Pillars of Hercules (Gibraltar) and dwelt for a long course of time in Spain among the most savage of tribes, but nowhere could they be subdued by any race, however barbarous. Thence they came (by way of Ireland) ... to their home in the West, where they still live today ... In their Kingdom there have reigned one hundred and thirteen Kings of their own Royal Stock, THE LINE UNBROKEN BY A SINGLE FOREIGNER.'**

In their Declaration these Scottish Leaders claim to have been the first to accept Christianity, saying:- **'That the King of Kings and Lord of Lords, our Lord Jesus Christ, after his Passion and Resurrection, called them, <u>even though settled in the uttermost part of the earth</u>, almost the first to His Most Holy Faith. Nor would he have confirmed them in that faith by merely anyone, but by the first of His Apostles by calling – though second or third in rank – the most gentle St. Andrew, the Blessed Peter's brother, and desired him to keep them under his protection as their patron forever.'**

Many of those one hundred and thirteen Kings mentioned in the Declaration were Kings of the Gael Sciot Iber in Spain, and many others in an unbroken line were Kings of Eri (Ireland) where they stayed for over a thousand years before migrating to Scotland.

<u>Lia Fail – Stone of Destiny</u>

Many of these Kings in an unbroken succession had been crowned upon the Lia-Fail (Stone of Destiny) or Jacob's Pillar Stone, which had been brought to Ireland by the Prophet Jeremiah, about 598 BC and upon which Eocaid and Tatla or Tephi, the Hebrew Princess – daughter of Zedekiah, had been crowned; healing the **'breach'** in the Zarah and Pharez lines of Judah's dynasty.

In the year 503 AD, one of the Irish Kings of this line, Fergus Mac Erca, moved the Stone of Beth-el, Jacob's Pillar Stone – to Iona. There it remained until 836 AD when King Kenneth moved it to Scone, where upon which all the Kings of Scotland were crowned. It remained in Scotland for almost eight hundred years, when in 1296 AD it was removed by King Edward I of England to London, where Edward had a special chair made for it – and placed in Westminster Abbey, now called the Coronation Chair, and upon which all the English Monarchs have been crowned in an unbroken succession.

The present Queen Elizabeth II being able to trace her regal line back through the English, Scottish and Irish Kings to the Royal Line of David and Solomon!

Concerning this stone, it has been written:-

> *'Unless the fates are faithless found*
>
> *And prophets voice be vain*
>
> *Where'er this sacred stone*
>
> *The Scottish race shall reign.'*

Sir Walter Scott

What had been done by Edward I in bringing the Lia-Fail to Westminster was completed by King James VI of Scotland, who was invited to become King of England in 1603 AD, assuming the title of King James I. By the wheel of destiny, the Monarchal Line of David was welded together in this action and the 'prophecy' in the rhyme fulfilled.

The Scottish Declaration of Independence

Drawn up by Bernard de Linton, Abbot of Aberbrothock and Chancellor of Scotland, and sent to Pope John XXII by the Scottish Estates in Parliament assembled in the Abbey of Aberbrothock, under the presidency of King Robert the Bruce, on April 6th A.D. 1320

Fig. 21: The Scottish Declaration of Independence – 6th April 1830 AD

The Scottish Declaration of Independence

Written in fluent Latin, the Declaration of Arbroath reads in English as follows:-

'To the Most Holy Father in Christ and Lord, the Lord John, by divine providence Supreme Pontiff of the Holy Roman and Universal Church, his humble and devout sons Duncan, Earl of Fife, Thomas Randolph, Earl of Moray, Lord of Man and of Annandale, Patrick Dunbar, Earl of March, Malise, Earl of Strathearn, Malcolm, Earl of Lennos, William, Earl of Ross, Magnus, Earl of Caithness and Orkney, and William, Earl of Sutherland; Walter, Steward of Scotland, William Soules, Butler of Scotland, James, Lord of Douglas, Roger Mowbray, David, Lord of Brechin, David Graham, Ingram Umfraville, John Mentaith, guardian of the earldom of Menteith, Alexander Fraser, Gilbert Hay, Constable of Scotland, Robert Keith, Marschal of Scotland, Henry St. Clair, John Graham, David Lindsay, William Oliphant, Patrick Graham, John Fenton, William Abernathy, David Wemyss, William Mushet, Fergus of Ardrossan, Eustace Maxwell, William Ramsay, William Mowat, Alan Murray, Donald Campbell, John Cameron, Reginald Cheyne, Alexander Seton, Andrew Leslie, and Alexander Straiton, and the other barons and freeholders and the whole community of the realm of Scotland send all manner of filial reverence, with devout kisses of his blessed feet.

Most Holy Father and Lord, we know and from the chronicles and books of the ancients we find that among other famous nations our own, the Scots, has been graced with widespread renown. They journeyed from Greater Scythia by way of the Tyrrhenian Sea and the Pillars of Hercules, and dwelt for a long course of time in Spain among the most savage tribes, but nowhere could they be subdued by any race, however barbarous.

Thence they came, twelve hundred years after the people of Israel crossed the Red Sea, to their home in the west where they still live today. The Britons they first drove out, the Picts they utterly destroyed, and even though very often assailed by the Norwegians, the Danes and the English, they took possession of that home with many victories and untold efforts; and, as the historians of old time bear witness, they have held it free of all bondage ever since. In their kingdom there have reigned one hundred and thirteen kings of their own royal stock, the line unbroken by a single foreigner.

The high qualities and deserts of these people, were they not otherwise manifest, gain glory enough from this: that the king of kings and Lord of lords, our Lord Jesus Christ, after His Passion and Resurrection, called them, even though settled in the uttermost parts of the earth, almost the first to His most holy faith.

Nor would he have them confirmed in that faith by merely anyone but by the first of His Apostles by calling – though second or third in rank – the most gentle Saint Andrew, the Blessed Peter's brother, and desired him to keep them under his protection as their patron forever.

The Most Holy Fathers your predecessors gave careful heed to these things and bestowed many favours and numerous privileges on this same kingdom and people, as being the special charge of the Blessed Peter's brother. Thus our nation under their protection did indeed live in freedom and peace up to the time when that mighty prince the King of the English, Edward, the father of the one who reigns today, when our kingdom had no head and our people harboured no malice or treachery and were then unused to wars or invasions, came in the guise of a friend and ally to harass them as an enemy.

The deeds of cruelty, massacre, violence, pillage, arson, imprisoning prelates, burning down monasteries, robbing and killing monks and nuns, and yet other outrages without number which he committed against our people, sparing neither age nor sex, religion nor rank, no one could describe nor fully imagine unless he had seen them with his own eyes.

But from these countless evils we have been set free, by the help of Him who though He afflicts yet heals and restores, by our most tireless Prince, King and Lord, the Lord Robert. He, that his people and his heritage might be delivered out of the hands of our enemies, met toil and fatigue, hunger and peril, like another Maccabaeus or Joshua, and bore them cheerfully. Him, too, divine providence, his right of succession according to our laws and customs which we shall maintain to the death, and the due consent and assent of us all have made our Prince and King.

To him, as to the man by whom salvation has been wrought unto our people, we are bound both by law and by his merits that our freedom may be still maintained, and by him, come what may, we mean to stand.

Yet if he should give up what he has begun, and agree to make us or our kingdom subject to the King of England or the English, we should exert ourselves at once to drive him out as our enemy and a subverter of his own rights and ours, and make some other man who was well able to defend us our King; for, as long as but a hundred of us remain alive, never will we on any conditions be brought under English rule. It is in truth not for glory, nor riches, nor honours that we are fighting, but for freedom – for that alone, which no honest man gives up but with life itself.

Therefore it is, Reverend Father and Lord, that we beseech your Holiness with our most earnest prayers and suppliant hearts, inasmuch as you will in your sincerity and goodness consider all this, that, since with Him whose vice-regent on earth you are there is neither weighing nor distinction of Jew and Greek,

Scotsman or Englishman, you will look with eyes of a father on the troubles and privations brought by the English upon us and upon the Church of God. May it please you to admonish and exhort the King of the English, who ought be satisfied with what belongs to him since England used once to be enough for seven kings or more, to leave us Scots in peace, who live in this poor little Scotland, beyond which there is no dwelling-place at all, and covet nothing but our own. We are sincerely willing to do anything for him, having regard to our condition, that we can, to win peace for ourselves.

This truly concerns you, Holy Father, since you see the savagery of the heathen raging against the Christians, as the sins of Christians have indeed deserved, and the frontiers of Christendom being pressed inward every day; and how much it will tarnish your holiness's memory if (which God forbid) the Church suffers eclipse or scandal in any branch of it during your time, you must perceive. Then rouse the Christian princes who for false reasons pretend that they cannot go to the help of the Holy Land because of wars they have on hand with their neighbours. The real reason that prevents them is that in making war on their smaller neighbours they find quicker profit and weaker resistance. But how cheerfully our Lord the King and we too would go there if the King of the English would leave us in peace, He from Whom nothing is hidden well knows; and we profess and declare it to you as the Vicar of Christ and to all Christendom.

But if your Holiness puts too much faith in the tales the English tell and will not give sincere belief to all this, nor refrain from favouring them to our prejudice, then the slaughter of bodies, the perdition of souls, and all the other misfortunes that will follow, inflicted on them by us and by us on them, will, we believe, be surely laid by the most High to your charge.

To conclude, we are and shall ever be, as far as duty calls us, ready to do your will in all things, as obedient sons to you as His Vicar; and to Him as the Supreme King and Judge, we commit the maintenance of our cause, casting our cares upon Him and firmly trusting that He will inspire us with courage and bring our enemies to nought.

May the Most High preserve you to His Holy Church in holiness and health and grant you length of days.

Given at the monastery of Arbroath in Scotland on the sixth day of the month of April in the year of grace thirteen hundred and twenty and the fifteenth year of the reign of our King aforesaid.'

CHAPTER **ELEVEN**

The American Connection

Indeed, not only did Kings of Scottish blood reign in England, but stout hearted Scots scattered all over the world, providing leadership in new countries forming abroad. Several Scots placed their signature to the 'U.S Declaration of Independence', among whom was Colonel George Ross. While he was placing his signature to that document, his brother John was fighting and dying to give effect to its brave words. And it was the widow of John Ross who sewed together the first flag of the United States, in the form of thirteen stars and thirteen stripes.

Beginning 1610 AD thousands of Eri people left the British Isles and settled in Colonies in North America. They entered the forests, cut down trees, and planted crops, built homes and farms, and created Communities which developed into Towns, some of which became Cities. They were at the forefront of the pioneers. They went under the 'Royal Charter of the Kings of England'. Many went to Canada in the North, and many to what is now the United States in the South. All of the first settlers came directly from Britain to North America, first the English, followed by the Welsh, the Scots and the Irish. The 1980 census taken in the United States show that the majority of their citizens trace their roots back to Britain.

Large numbers came from other Israelite Nations such as Denmark, Norway, Holland, Sweden. And other descendants came from Germany, France and other European Countries.

Although Canada and the United States appear to be a conglomerate of many people, they primarily have their roots in the Twelve Tribes of Israel, and fulfil the prophecy made by Jacob concerning his grandsons Ephraim and Manasseh, the twin sons of Joseph.

The United States undoubtedly fulfils the prophecies for Manasseh and Canada, being also one of the **'Young lions thereof'** – is clearly the American portion of Ephraim. These two Great Nations of North America have lived for over two hundred years on each side of an open, unfortified border. Of course there have been differences between them; but they have always been able to settle these by arbitration. They are Model Nations for the future development of Nations in the Worldwide Political Kingdom of God, soon to be established upon the earth.

American and British Roots Are in the Bible

In seeking their roots the people of America should turn to the Bible. They should listen to the words of Isaiah:-

> *'Hearken to me, ye that follow after righteousness, ye that seek the Lord: look unto the rock whence ye are hewn .... look unto Abraham your father, and unto Sarah that bear you: for I called him alone, and blessed him, and increased him.'*

Let them look at the Ten Tribes of Israel in particular, those that had separated themselves from Judah and Jerusalem, and formed a separate Nation to the North.

God – Jehovah had looked upon these people as his wife. The 'Marriage Contract' had been entered into at Sinai and sealed by the **'blood of the covenant'** (EXODUS 24: 7-8). Metaphorically speaking it was a marriage in every sense of the word – both parties were bound by the contract. Jehovah as the 'husband' and Israel as the 'wife'. This is a difficult concept to accept for most Christians, but once it is understood the Scriptures are made that much clearer, and the reason for the crucifixion and shed blood of Christ, and the atonement much more understandable.

His 'wife' constantly committed adultery with other Gods (JER 3: 6-14). For this reason the 'husband' issued a bill of divorce.

He sent his messenger HOSEA to plead with them to change their ways, he warns them of impending judgements for their sins, making it clear that they would not escape punishment if they persisted in transgressing the commandments, statutes, and judgements of God. Both HOSEA and Isaiah looked forward to the coming deliverance when the unfaithful wife would be forgiven and the bill of divorcement blotted out. ISAIAH 54: 5-10 and 53: 1-8. There is no question in these Scriptures regarding the relationship between Israel and Jehovah – he was the 'HUSBAND', she was the wayward wife. She was the 'WOMAN' forsaken and causing grief to her husband, but he loved her still and promised not to forsake her completely, for he was also her Redeemer Jesus Christ, the Holy One of Israel.

It was primarily for Israel's transgression that Jesus Christ paid the penalty. The Law which He gave to Israel at Sinai demanded the punishment of death for adultery which we are told 'she' committed. However, the whole nation could not die, and it is not possible for one who had sinned to redeem himself or herself, so for this purpose a Redeemer was required.

> *'But he was wounded for our (Israel's) transgressions, he was bruised for our (Israel's) iniquities; the chastisement of our (Israel's) peace was upon him; and by his stripes we are healed ......' (verse 5)*

> *'For the transgressions of my people (Israel) was he stricken ......' (verse 8).*

Can we ever understand the condescension of God's love? After all that his 'wife', Israel, had done, playing the harlot and committing adultery with false Gods, not once or twice, but hundreds of times, he was willing to forgive her – willing to die for her, and take her back in a new betrothal. (JEREMIAH 31: 31-34, HOSEA 2: 19-20)

> *'Therefore, behold, I will allure her, and bring her into the wilderness and speak comfortably unto her. And I will give her*

vineyards from thence, and the valley of Achor for a door of hope and she shall sing there, as in the days of her youth, and as in the day when she came out of the land of Egypt.'

(HOSEA 2: 14-15)

The **'door of hope'** which God has offered his people is the atoning sacrifice at Calvary.

Jehovah, through Hosea refers to rejected, divorced Israel as **'LO-RUHAMAH'**, (not having obtained mercy) and **'LO-AMMI'** (not my people) (HOSEA 1: 6-10)

Then because of the **'door of hope'**- the Lord refers to them as **'AMMI'** meaning:- my people, and **'RUHAMAH'** meaning:- having obtained mercy.

'And <u>I will sow her unto me in the earth</u>; and I will have mercy upon her that had not obtained mercy; and I will say unto them which were not my people, Thou art my people; and they shall say, Thou art my God.'

(HOSEA 2: 23, 1: 10)

In the very names of their Nations, both the British and American peoples are identified as Israel.

The word 'BRITH' in Hebrew means:- 'Covenant' – the 'h' being silent, it would be pronounced 'BRIT'. The word 'ISH' in Hebrew denotes man or people. The whole being 'BRIT-ISH' or Covenant people.

The word SAXONS being a derivative of I-SAACS-SONS or 'SONS OF ISAAC'. **'For in Isaac shall thy seed be called'** (GEN 21: 12).

Also the name AMERICA reveals its people's true identity – AM-ERI-CA. The first two letters, a shortened version of 'AMMI' means:- **'MY PEOPLE'**. They were also called 'RUHAMAH', which means:- 'HAVING OBTAINED MERCY'. They have obtained mercy and become the People of God, through the **'door of hope'**. By benefitting from the Sacrifice of Christ upon the Cross at Calvary, both America and Canada have become the two Christian Nations before the World. **'AM'** my people. **'RUHAMAH'** who have obtained mercy.

The central three letters of AM-ERI-CA is the exact name of Eri people, or the **'hero people'** of God, who are all descended from Shem, the birthright son of Noah.

They were formed for a definite purpose, and have had the direct and divine protection of God in their long wanderings across the face of the earth ..... **'I will sow her unto me in the earth, and I will have mercy upon her'**. They have loved freedom and are, with the other Anglo-Saxon Celtic Nations, the leading Nations of the Free World. As ERI-ANS they are of the ARYAN race, which is the phonetic spelling of the original word ERI-ANS.

The ending of the word AM-ERI-CA means the place where the ERI people are found. 'C' for Canada, 'A' for America.

On MERCATOR'S WORLD MAP of 1538 AD, America is not shown by that name, but 'AMERI'! (AM-ERI) 'AM' = My People of ERI. This map is displayed in a book called <u>'Maps of the Ancient Sea Kings – by Charles H. Hapgood – Turnstone Books – 37 Upper Addison Gardens – London W14.</u>

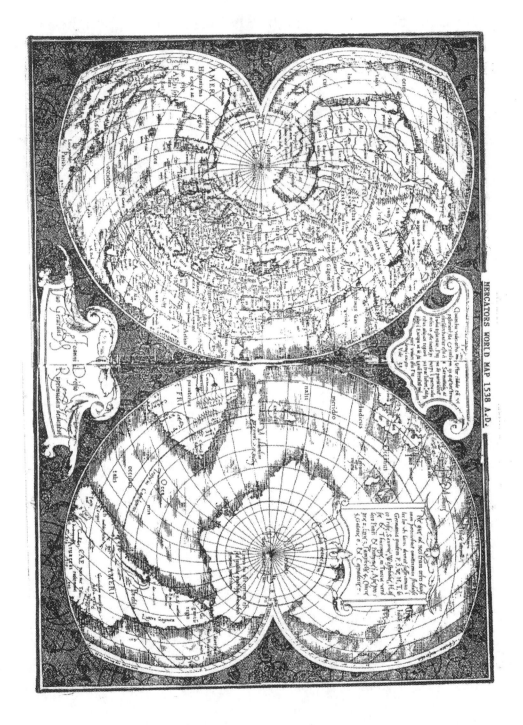

Fig. 22: Mercators World Map

Inherited Blessings

By relating the blessings given by God to <u>ABRAHAM</u> – <u>ISAAC</u> – <u>JACOB</u> – and by Jacob to his two grandsons <u>EPHRAIM</u> and <u>MANASSEH</u> to the facts of history, we can readily see that the Nations of Great Britain and the Commonwealth, and America and Canada are a fulfilment of those blessings.

To Abraham the Lord said:-

> *'And I will make of thee a 'GREAT' nation;*
>
> *And I will bless thee and MAKE THY NAME GREAT;*
>
> *And thou shalt be a blessing;*
>
> *And I will bless them that bless thee, and*
>
> *Curseth them that curseth thee;*
>
> *And in thee all the families of the earth will be blessed.'*

(GENESIS 12: 2-3)

Surely this prophecy has literally been fulfilled for the only Nation on earth to have the pre-fix 'GREAT' to its name is Great Britain, with its Empire, now a Commonwealth representing the fantastic geographical blessings, making it literally a 'Great' Nation. **'And in these all the families of the earth will be blessed.'**

In this prophecy we see the spiritual blessings which the world would receive through the colonizing efforts of Israel, mingling the blood of Abraham within all Nations, and in a more important way being the instruments in proclaiming the Gospel of Salvation to all peoples through the restoration of the true Church and Priesthood.

In blessing Jacob the Lord said:-

> *'And God said unto him, thy name is Jacob; thy name shall not be called any more Jacob, but ISRAEL shall be thy name: And he called his name ISRAEL.*
>
> *And God said unto him, I am God Almighty: be fruitful and multiply; A NATION, AND A COMPANY OF NATIONS, shall be of thee, and Kings shall come out of thy loins.'*

(GENESIS 35: 10-11)

So from Jacob was to come:-

1. A singular Great Nation.

2. A company (Commonwealth) of Nations.

(EPHESIANS 2: 12)

A prophecy fulfilled in the two Israelite Nations of Great Britain and her Commonwealth, and the United States of America.

In the forty eighth Chapter of Genesis is recorded Jacob's blessings upon his grandsons Ephraim and Manasseh. When Jacob blessed the sons of Joseph he was under the necessity of crossing his arms in order that he might place his right hand, from which the blessings of the birthright would come, upon the head of Ephraim, the one whom the spirit had designated as the birthright inheritor, and his left hand upon the head of Manasseh. Ephraim was the youngest of the two boys. Joseph tried to correct Jacob in this action reminding him that Manasseh was the firstborn.

'And his father refused, and said, I know it my son, I know it: He (Manasseh) shall also become a GREAT PEOPLE (Singular Great Nation), and he also shall be GREAT: But truly his brother (Ephraim) shall be GREAT<u>ER</u> THAN HE (Manasseh) and his (Ephraim's) seed shall become a multitude (Commonwealth) of Nations.'

(GENESIS 48: 19)

And so we see that what in fact took place in this action was that Jacob had transferred his own blessing given him by Almighty God – upon the heads of his grandsons Ephraim and Manasseh and their descendants.

And in the crossing of his hands, Jacob necessarily made the sign of the Celtic Cross (X). This is the Celtic pre-Christian Cross of which relics are found wherever Israel travelled. This 'sign' is found in what is known as the 'Union Jack' – the British National Flag, and the same sign is found in the ensign of the British Royal Navy Vessels. The sign is also buried in the very name SAXON, which is a shortened version of the name ISAAC or ISAAC-SONS = SAXONS, a blessing given to Isaac by God even before his birth.

'For in Isaac shall thy seed be called' (GENESIS 21: 12). Also to be found in the 'Union Jack' is the Christian Cross + of Christ. Let us not spiritualise away national things, nor nationalise spiritual things. Let us understand the sacred word of God as it is.

Jacob had also received a further blessing:-

'And thy seed shall be as the dust of the Earth, and thou shalt spread abroad to the WEST (America), and to the EAST (India), and to the NORTH (Canada), and to the SOUTH (Australia/ New Zealand).'

(GENESIS 28: 14)

Is not this a marvellous revelation?

> *'Thus saith the Lord, in an acceptable time, have I heard thee, and in a day of Salvation have I helped thee. And I will preserve thee, and give thee for a covenant of the people, TO ESTABLISH THE EARTH, TO CAUSE TO INHERIT THE DESOLATE HERITAGES.'*

> (ISAIAH 49: 8)

The acceptable time for Great Britain's growth as an Empire Nation began in the fifteenth century. Through the previous centuries this Island Nation had been preserved, and is still preserved from the aspirations of those who attempted invasion and subjugation of its people, except those who were part of God's overall plan for His Israel people, in the Isles of the Sea.

The Day of Salvation, referred to the ending of Israel's period of chastisement, the seven times punishment period i.e. 2,520 years (LEVITICUS 26), which extended from the time of Israel's captivity into Assyria 721 BC to 1800 AD.

The nation was preserved for the purpose of colonizing the 'DESOLATE PLACES' of the earth.

Britain's colonizing activities followed the exact way in which God had said i.e. firstly to the WEST – America being the first colonizing effort in the sixteen hundreds. Then to the EAST – India. NORTH – to Canada, and finally SOUTH to Australia and New Zealand.

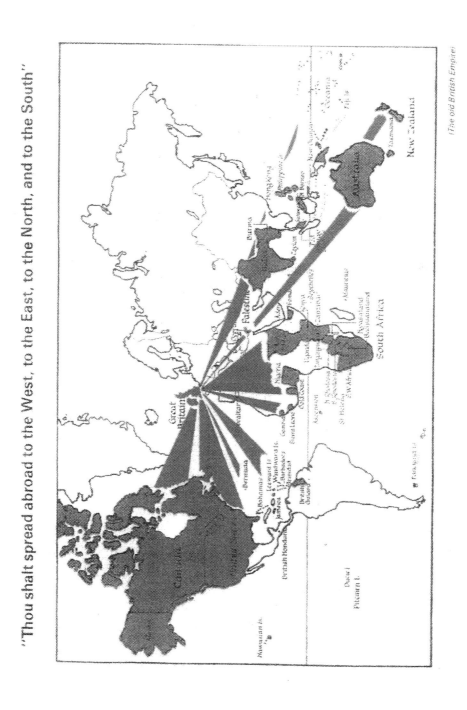

Fig. 23: Picture: The Old British Empire

In this new Island Home, the 'House of Israel' was to be called by a new name, they were no longer to be called 'ISRAEL'.

> *'And the gentiles shall see thy righteousness, and all Kings of Glory: and thou shalt be called by a new name, which the mouth of the Lord shall name.'*

(ISAIAH 62: 2)

The name by which Israel became known is BRITISH or SAXON. BRITISH being a composition of two Hebrew words, BRITH = Covenant, and ISH = man, i.e. 'Covenant People'.

These two nations, descendants of Ephraim and Manasseh were to inherit all of the Sea Gates of the Earth, promised to their Great Progenitor – Abraham.

> *'And thy seed shall possess the gate of his enemies.'*

(GENESIS 22: 16-17)

This prophecy was also fulfilled, for, between them Great Britain and the United States of America have at one time or another held all the 'sea gates' of this earth, i.e. GIBRALTAR, MALTA, SUEZ, ADEN, SINGAPORE, HONG KONG, CAPE OF GOOD HOPE, THE FALKLANDS, PANAMA, HAWAII, THE PHILLIPINES. And in keeping with the prophecy these have been mostly, if not all in, or near, Territories and Nations who have not been friendly, in fact, quite the opposite!

After the Tribes of Israel had settled in their new Island Home, and had eventually repulsed Roman and other invaders, their numbers began to increase and they began to say, **'this place is too small, such a small island cannot support us all'**. So between 1500 AD and 1800 AD they began to colonize. The prophet ISAIAH foresaw these events 1000 years – (millennia) previously. He states:-

'For thy waste and desolate places, and the land of thy 'exile',
shall even now be too narrow by reason of the inhabitants, and
they that swallowed thee up shall be far away.'

(ISAIAH 49: 19)

It was Assyria who had **'swallowed up'** the nation of Israel. But here in the land of their **'exile' (The British Islands)** the Assyrians would be **'far away'.** However, the islands were too small to support a growing population, and so the work of colonizing began, if it had not commenced this island would now be attempting to support all of the Populations of British Origin in the White Commonwealth, and those of the United States and Canada!

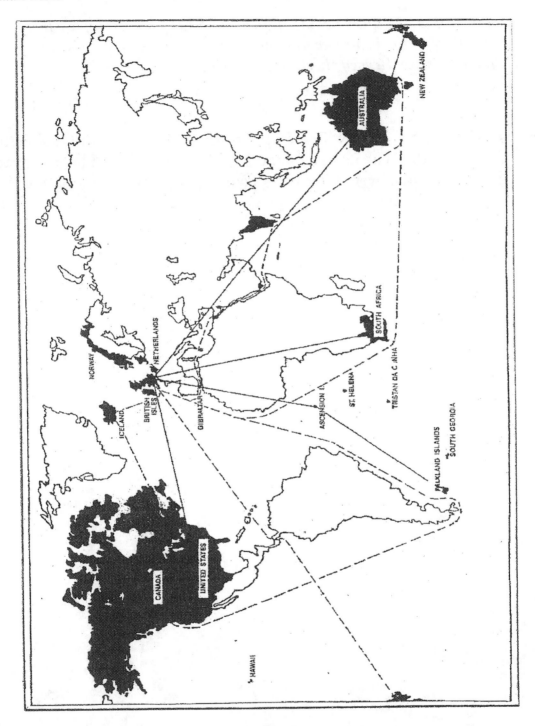

Fig. 24: Map: Israel's Sea Gates

Then Isaiah continues:-

> *'The children which thou shalt have, after thou hast lost the other (Colony) shall <u>say again</u> in thine ears, the place is too strait for me: give me place that I may dwell'.*

(ISAIAH 49: 20)

The first Major Colony which the British acquired was the American Colonies, which they eventually lost in the American War of Independence 1776 AD. Therefore 'AGAIN' it became necessary for the Island Israel People to seek new Colonies, which they did, firstly to the East in India, then to the North in Canada, and finally to South Africa, Australia, and New Zealand.

Isaiah also informs the 'Children of Israel' in the Islands:-

> *'Is my hand shortened that it cannot redeem'.*

(ISAIAH 50: 2)

> *'Look unto the rock whence ye are hewn, and to the hole of the pit whence ye are digged ..... the isles shall wait upon me, and on my arm shall they trust.'*

(ISAIAH 51: 1-5)

Then in Chapters Fifty Three and Fifty Four, God expresses Divine Love for his People Israel:-

> *'For the mountains shall depart, and the hills be removed; but my kindness shall not depart from thee, neither shall my covenant of peace be removed, saith the Lord that hath mercy on thee.'*

(ISAIAH 54: 10)

The covenant with God made with Abraham, Isaac and Jacob was unconditional, and God would not, could not, ever annul it, however, they could be punished, which they were, but when the period of chastisement came to an end in 1800 AD the Lord began to emancipate his people.

> *'In righteousness thou shalt be established: thou shalt be far from oppression; for thou shalt not fear, and from terror, for it shall not come near thee.*
>
> *Behold they shall surely gather together, but not by me: Whosoever shall gather together against thee shall fall for thy sake ..... No weapon that is formed against thee shall prosper; and every tongue that shall rise against thee in judgement thou shalt condemn. This is the heritage of the servants of the Lord, and their righteousness is of me, saith the Lord.'*

> (ISAIAH 54: 14-17)

This is about as clear as it could be. The Lord is not speaking of a Church here, he is speaking to his New Born Nation of Israel, in the Isles of Britain and America, and it is significant that since 1800 AD, no Nation has been successful in their attempts to subjugate our Nations. Isaiah gives us an insight to the growth of this Island Nation and the **'lost colony'** of America.

> *'A little one shall become a thousand, and a small one a strong nation: I the Lord will hasten it in his time.'*

> (ISAIAH 60: 22)

The **'little one'** that grew into **'a thousand'** or Empire and Commonwealth, were the British.

The **'small one'** (Colony) which was lost and became a strong singular **'Great'** Nation is the United States of America.

> *'Thy sun shall no more go down; neither shall thy moon withdraw itself: for the Lord shall be thine everlasting light, and the days of thy mourning shall be ended.'*

> (ISAIAH 60: 20)

Was there not a saying that **'the sun never sets on the British Empire'**, and after 1800 AD her **'days of mourning'**, (2,520 years) were surely ended.

> *'For ye are my witnesses, saith the Lord, and my servant whom I have chosen ..... this people (Israel), have I formed for myself; they shall shew forth my praise.'*

(ISAIAH 43: 10, 21)

These witnesses are nothing to do with a Church, <u>any Church</u>, but purely a message to God's Covenant Nation, informing them of their great commission.

After the period of chastisement was ended in 1800 AD, the redemption took effect, and the Lord restored the everlasting Gospel to the Earth, and the true authority to administer the ordinances represented by the Melchezedek Priesthood, which would once again be manifest in Israel.

> *'But ye shall be named Priests of the Lord, men shall call you the Ministers of our God: Ye shall eat the riches of the Gentiles ..... and I will direct their work in truth, and I will make AN EVERLASTING COVENANT with them.*
>
> *And their seed shall be known among the Gentiles, and their offspring among the people: and all that see them shall acknowledge them, that they are the seed which the Lord hath blessed.*
>
> *I will greatly rejoice in the Lord, my soul shall be joyful in my God; for he hath clothed me with the 'garments of salvation', he hath covered me with the 'robe of righteousness', as a bridegroom decketh himself with ornaments, and as a bride adorneth herself with her jewels.'*

(ISAIAH 61: 8-10)

This is just about one of the most sublime statements in the whole of the 'Book of Israel'.

What a revelation these verses portray.

The Priest of the Lord, those who hold the true Priesthood will be recognized by <u>all</u> people, I think that is true of Mormon Missionaries, even though they dress like others, somehow people 'just know' who they are.

'I will direct their work in truth', can only refer to the true restored gospel.

I will make **'an everlasting covenant'** with them, this also has been fulfilled, and he has in that **'everlasting covenant'** clothed his servants with **'GARMENTS OF SALVATION'** and a **'ROBE OF RIGHTEOUSNESS'**.

In this brief exposition on Isaiah, are not our eyes now to be opened? That this is the Lord's message to our peoples of Great Britain and America, surely this must be so with so much weight of evidence. In one bold sweep across the centuries both HOSEA and ISAIAH tell the story of the rejection, the punishment, redemption, and ultimate restoration of the 'House of Israel'.

Hosea's whole message is central to this theme. Isaiah introduces his message in Chapter Twenty Four, then from Chapter Forty through to Chapter Sixty Five his whole message is to the Hebrew-Israel people, descendants of SHEM-EBER-ABRAHAM-ISAAC and JACOB, **'In the Isles of the Sea'**, and their descendants throughout the World.

Finally the Lord says:-

'Who is blind, but my servant? or deaf as my messenger that I sent? Who is blind as he that is perfect, and blind as the Lord's servant?'

It is not the servants of God who hold the true Priesthood which are blind, it is not the true Church which is blind.

It is our Nations of Britain and America, and the other Anglo-Saxon Celtic Nations in the Earth, they are blind, BLIND TO THEIR TRUE IDENTITY.

Paul said:-

'For I would not brethren, that ye should be ignorant of this mystery, lest ye should be wise in your own conceits; that blindness in part is happened to Israel, until the fullness of the Gentiles be come in'.

The fullness of the Gentiles has now come in, and Israel's blindness is being removed.

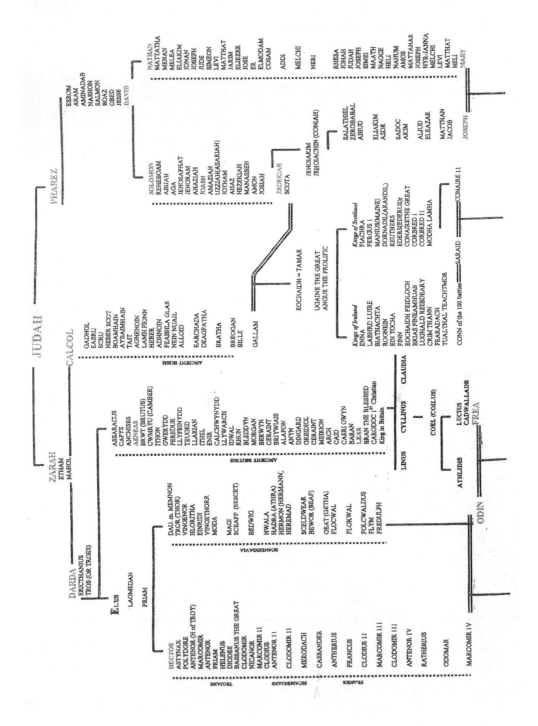

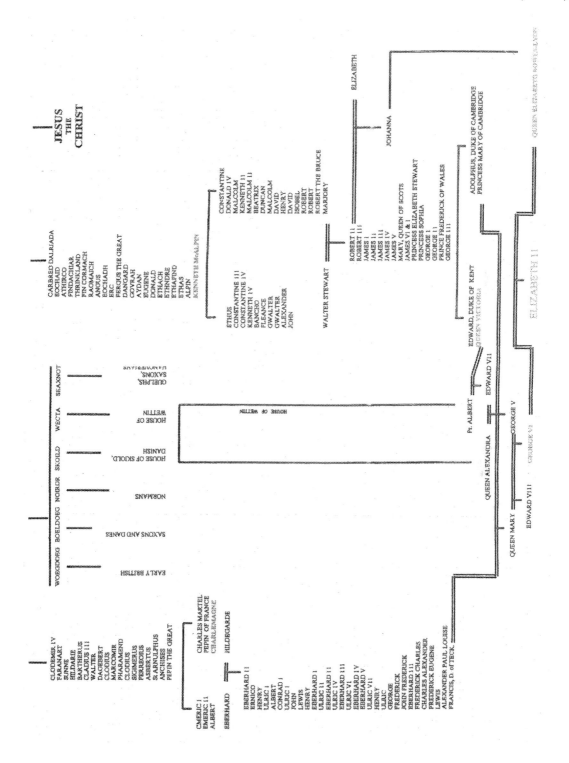

The Coronation Chair

The Stone of Destiny, upon which the Kings and Queens in England, Scotland and Ireland have been anointed and before in biblical times; by tradition it is the stone upon which Jacob laid his head at Bethel to be given the prophetic Kingdom vision *(Genesis 28:10-22).*

Scriptural References
Israel in the Isles of the Sea

<u>ISAIAH</u>

11: 11

13: 22

20: 6

23: 2

24: 15-16

28: 11

33: 13, 16-19

34: 14

40: 1-2, 15, 31

41: 1, 5, 8, 10

42: 4, 10, 12, 15

49: 1

51: 5

59: 18

60: 9

66: 19

<u>OTHER REFERENCES</u>

JEREMIAH 31: 10

EZEKIEL 26: 15, 18

27: 3, 6-7, 15, 35

39: 6

DANIEL 11: 18

PSALMS 72: 10

97: 1

BIBLIOGRAPHY

J.S.T BIBLE – DICTIONARY AND TOPICAL GUIDE...........

ANALYTICAL CONCORDANCE OF THE BIBLE .... YOUNG

ENCYCLOPAEDIA BRITANNICA ....

JOSEPHUS – COMPLETE WORKS .... Translated by

Wm WHISTON A.M

HISTORY OF IRELAND .... MOORE

CHRONICLES OF IRELAND (ERI)...................... Translated by

DR R O'CONNOR

ANNALS OF THE KINGDOM OF IRELAND – BY THE FOUR MASTERS -
(One Volume Translated by JOHN O'DONOVAN)

TRIADS OF THE CYMRY ....

HISTORY OF SCOTLAND .... REV. J A WYLIE L.L.D

HISTORY OF SCOTLAND .... T WRIGHT

THE ANGLO SAXON CHRONICLES..............................

HISTORIA BRITANNICA ....CAMDEN

HISTORY OF THE ANGLO SAXONS.............. SHARON TURNER

THE PENGUIN ATLAS OF ANCIENT HISTORY (1967)......C McEVEDY

BRITISH HISTORY TRACED . . . . ROBERTS

ANDERSONS ROYAL GENEALOGIES . . . .

MISSING LINKS DISCOVERED IN ASSYRIAN TABLETS . . . .

E RAYMOND CAPT. M.A.

TRACING OUR ANCESTORS . . . . FREDERICK HABERMAN

PRE-HISTORIC LONDON – ITS MOUNDS AND CIRCLES . . . .

E O GORDON

CELT – DRUID AND CULDEE . . . . ISOBEL HILL ELDER

HISTORY OF THE DRUIDS . . . . J TOLAND

WESTMINSTER ABBEY . . . . PITKIN PICTORIALS

THE ROYAL LINE OF SUCCESSION . . . . P W MONTAGUE SMITH

PITKIN PICTORIALS

SYMBOLS OF OUR CELTO SAXON HERITAGE . . . . W H BENNETT

JACOB'S PILLAR . . . . E RAYMOND CAPT. M.A.

MAPS OF THE ANCIENT SEA KINGS . . . . CHARLES H HAPGOOD

Turnstone Books – 37 Upper Addison Gardens – London W14